NATIONAL GEOGRAPHIC
Reach™
Language • Literacy • Content

 NATIONAL GEOGRAPHIC 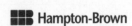 Hampton-Brown

Acknowledgments and credits continue on the inside back cover.
National Geographic and the Yellow Border are registered trademarks of the National Geographic Society.

National Geographic School Publishing
Hampton-Brown
www.NGSP.com

Printed in the USA.
DB Hess, Woodstock, IL

ISBN: 978-0-7362-7459-3

11 12 13 14 15 16 17 18 19   10 9 8 7 6 5 4 3 2

HPS230023

Contents

Unit 3: Water for Everyone

Unit 4: Lend a Hand

Unit 5: Everything Changes

Unit 6: Better Together

Unit 7: Best Buddies

Unit 8: Our United States

Name _____   Date _____

Hello, Neighbor!

Make a concept map with the answers to the Big Question: What is a community?

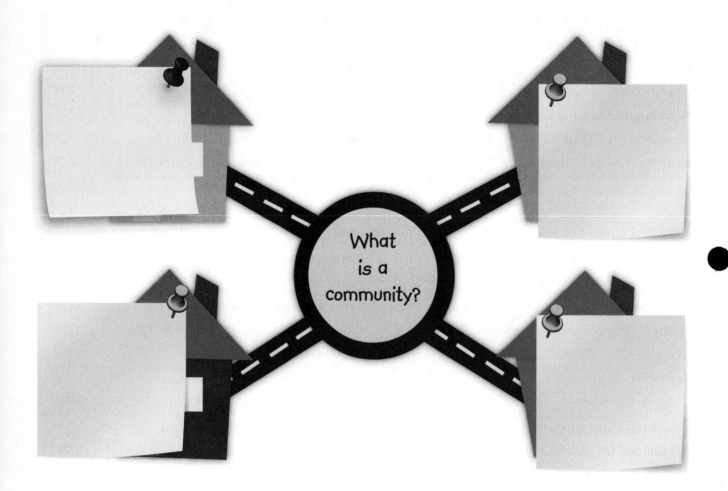

Name _____ Date _____

Character

Make a character map for Jae and Vera from the song "Our Hometown Workers."

Character	Who the Character Is	What the Character's Job Is

 Share your character map with a partner.

1.2

Name _____ Date _____

On the Job

Grammar Rules Nouns

A noun names a person, a place, or a thing.

Person	Place	Thing
cousin	park	flower
girl	garden	smile

Categorize the nouns.

My <u>uncle</u> takes me to his <u>shop</u>. He fixes <u>cars</u> in the <u>garage</u>. Our <u>neighbor</u> works there, too. I want to help, so I bring them the <u>tools</u> that they need. What a fun <u>job</u>!

Nouns		
Person	**Place**	**Thing**
uncle		

 Use three of the nouns above. Tell a partner something about you.

Name _____   Date _____

Quinito's Neighborhood

1

Quinito's mother is a carpenter. His father is a nurse.

2

He knows his other neighbors. They are a baker, a dentist, and a teacher. They are all busy.

3

Quinito is busy, too! He tells his teacher that his mother is a carpenter and his father is a nurse.

© NGSP & HB

Grammar: Singular and Plural Nouns

A Walk in the Park

Grammar Rules Plural Nouns

	Singular	Plural
• Add **-s** to most nouns.	game	game**s**
• Add **-es** to nouns that end in **x**, **ch**, **sh**, **ss**, **z**, and sometimes **o**.	box	box**es**
• For nouns that end in **-y**, change the **y** to **i** and then add **-es**.	party	part**ies**

Make the nouns plural.

Today, Marisa and I walked to the park. Marisa wanted to

play on the ___*swings*___ . Then we sat on the _____ to eat our
      (swing)   (bench)

_____ . I brought _____ to share. Then our _____
(snack)   (strawberry)   (friend)

came. We played under the blue _____ for hours. What a
                                   (sky)

great day!

 Pick two plural nouns from above and write new sentences. Read them to a partner.

© NGSP & HB

Name _____ Date _____

Quinito's Neighborhood

Make a character map for the people in "Quinito's Neighborhood."

Character	Who the Character Is	What the Character's Job Is
Mami and Papi	Quinito's parents	She is a carpenter. He is a nurse.
Guillermo	Quninto's neighbor	
Dona Estrella		She is a seamstress.

  Use your character map to describe the characters in "Quinito's Neighborhood" to a partner.

Name _____ Date _____

Use this passage to practice reading with proper intonation.

Quinito's Neighborhood

I am a very busy person, too.   7

I have to tell Mr. Gómez that my *mami*   16

is a carpenter and my *papi* is a nurse.   25

Intonation

B ☐ Does not change pitch.   A ☐ Changes pitch to match some of the content.

I ☐ Changes pitch, but does not match content.   AH ☐ Changes pitch to match all of the content.

Accuracy and Rate Formula

Use the formula to measure a reader's accuracy and rate while reading aloud.

_____ − _____ = _____
words attempted   number of errors   words correct per minute
in one minute   (wcpm)

Name _____   Date _____

Reading Options: Prediction Chart

Working Her Way Around the World

Fill out the prediction chart as you read.

What I know about Annie Griffiths Belt's job	What I think I will learn

 Tell a partner what new job you learned about.

© NGSP & HB

Name _____   Date _____

Compare Genres

Show how realistic fiction and a photo-essay are different.

Realistic Fiction	Photo-Essay
• tells about things that could really happen	• uses photographs and text to tell about a topic

 Take turns with a partner. Give information about a story or a photo-essay.

© NGSP & HB

The Make-It-Plural Game

1. **Play with a partner.**

2. **Spin the spinner.**

3. **Change the noun to a plural noun. Say a sentence using the plural noun.**

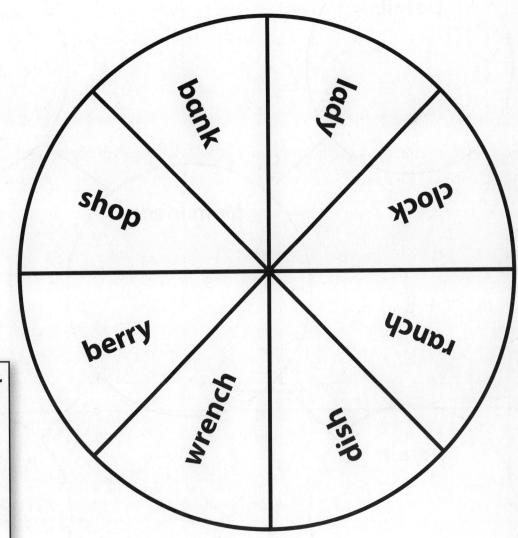

Make a Spinner

1. Put a paper clip ⚲ in the center of the circle.

2. Hold one end of the paper clip with a pencil.

3. Spin the paper clip around the pencil.

© NGSP & HB

For use with TE p. T31a   **1.10**   **Unit 1** | Hello, Neighbor!

Name _____ Date _____

Our Community

Make a details cluster to tell about places in your community.

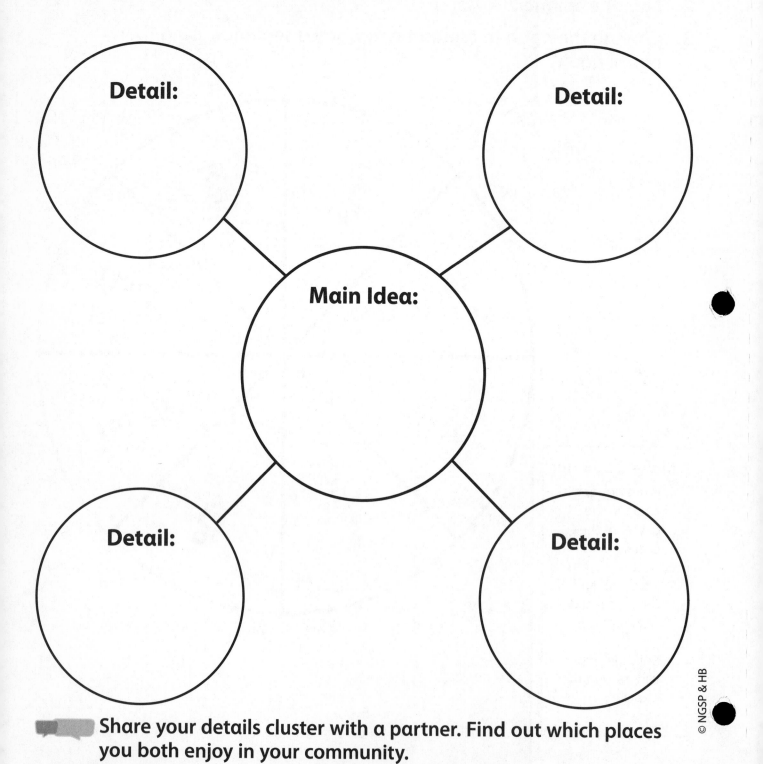

Detail:

Detail:

Main Idea:

Detail:

Detail:

Share your details cluster with a partner. Find out which places you both enjoy in your community.

© NGSP & HB

Name _____ Date _____

Places To Go

Grammar: Proper Nouns

- A **common noun** names a person, place, or thing.
  (Example: *hospital*)
- A **proper noun** names a specific person, place, or thing. Each proper noun begins with a capital letter.
  (Example: *Mercy Hospital*)

Categorize the nouns.

Ezra wants to go to the park. First, he must do his homework. He must read *Charlotte's Web*. He can find this book at Oak Public Library. The library is on King Street.

Common Nouns	Proper Nouns
park	Ezra

 Tell a partner the name of the street, city, and state where you live. Use proper nouns.

Name _____ Date _____

Be My Neighbor

A neighborhood is a special place where you live and learn. You play and work in a neighborhood.

Neighborhoods have places to play and shop. They have places to work and celebrate.

Neighbors share the place where they live. It's the place you call home.

Grammar: Possessive Nouns

Make-It-Possessive Game

Grammar Rules Possessive Nouns

Make a noun possessive by adding an apostrophe (') plus *-s* to the end. (Example: Sam's)

1. **Play with a partner.**

2. **Flip a coin.**

    Move 1 space.

    Move 2 spaces.

3. **Change the noun to a possessive noun. Say a sentence using the possessive noun.**

4. **The player who finishes first wins.**

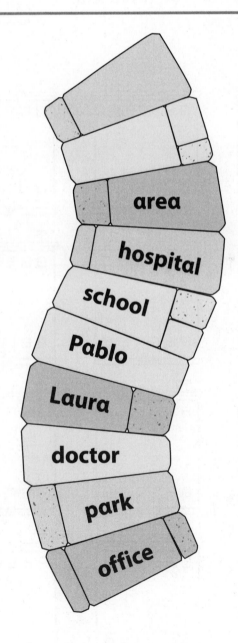

area

hospital

school

Pablo

Laura

doctor

park

office

© NGSP & HB

Vocabulary: Apply Word Knowledge

Vocabulary Bingo

1. Write one Key Word in each building.

2. Listen to the clues. Find the Key Word and use a marker to cover it.

3. Say "Bingo" when you have four markers in a row.

Key Words	
area	locate
building	park
home	place
hospital	population
identify	school
library	

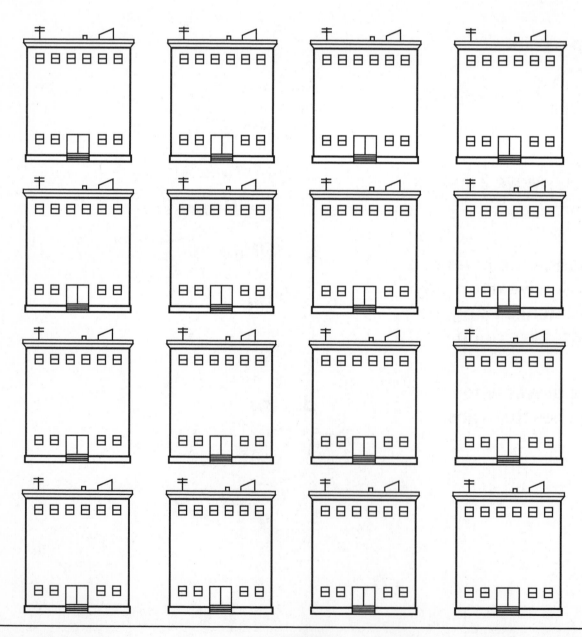

© NGSP & HB

Name _____ Date _____

Be My Neighbor

Make a details cluster for "Be My Neighbor." Look for details that tell more about the main idea.

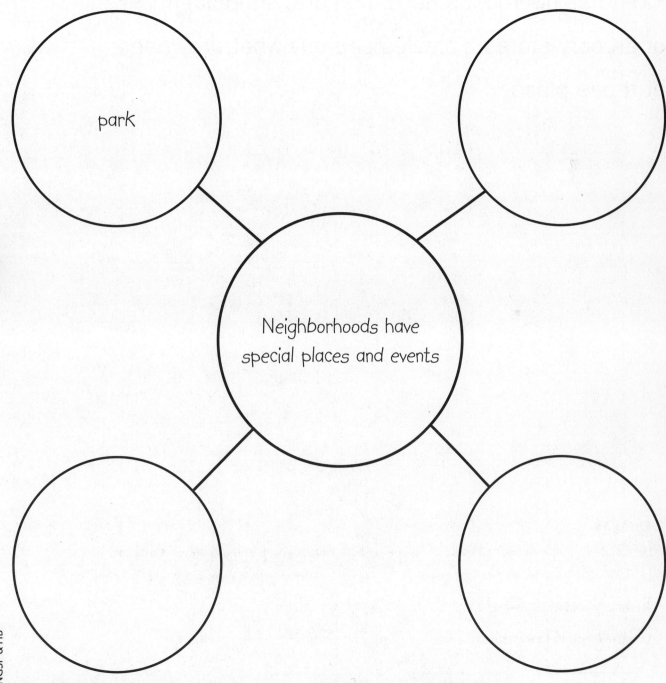

park

Neighborhoods have special places and events

💬 **Tell a partner about the main idea and details in "Be My Neighbor."**

© NGSP & HB

Name _____   Date _____

Use this passage to practice reading with proper phrasing.

Be My Neighbor

Most neighborhoods have markets, shopping malls,   6

or grocery stores. Families can buy what they need   15

at these places.   18

Phrasing

B ☐ Rarely pauses while reading the text.   A ☐ Frequently pauses at appropriate points in the text.

I ☐ Occasionally pauses while reading the text.   AH ☐ Consistently pauses at all appropriate points in the text.

Accuracy and Rate Formula

Use the formula to measure a reader's accuracy and rate while reading aloud.

_____ − _____ = _____
words attempted   number of errors   words corrected per
in one minute   minute (wcpm)

© NGSP & HB

Name _____ Date _____

My Favorite Place

Fill out the reflection journal as you read "My Favorite Place."

Page	My Questions	The Answers

  Discuss what you wrote in your reflection journal with your teacher.

Compare Media

Use this chart to compare "Be My Neighbor" and "My Favorite Place."

	Photo-Essay	Internet Bulletin Board
has photos	✓	✓
has captions		
has more than one writer		
gives facts		
asks and answers questions		
lets people share ideas and communicate		

 Take turns with a partner. Ask each other questions about a photo-essay or an Internet bulletin board.

© NGSP & HB

Name _____   Date _____

Grammar: Proper and Possessive Nouns

A Day in the Park

Grammar Rules Proper and Possessive Nouns

- A proper noun names a specific person, place, or thing. (Example: Texas)
- Some titles of people begin with a capital letter and end with a period. (Example: Dr.)
- A possessive noun names an owner. (Example: Jackson's)

Underline the proper nouns and write them in the chart. Then make each proper noun possessive. The first one is done for you.

<u>Mrs. Preston</u> lives in a neighborhood called Grandview. Her home is on Maple Street. Adam Preston is her son. We go to the same school. He is on my soccer team, too. Mr. Mohr is our coach.

Proper Nouns	Proper Possessive Nouns
Mrs. Preston	Mrs. Preston's

 Write a sentence with a proper noun and a proper possessive noun. Read your sentence to a partner.

For use with TE p. T59a   **1.20**   **Unit 1** | Hello, Neighbor!

© NGSP & HB

Name _____   Date _____

Focus and Coherence

	Are the Ideas Related?	Is the Writing Complete?
4 Wow!	All ideas are about one topic.	There is a beginning and an end. All of the details in the middle are important.
3 Ahh.	Most of the ideas are about one topic.	There is a beginning and an end. Most of the details in the middle are important.
2 Hmm.	There are many ideas that don't go together. It is hard to tell what the writing is about.	The writing has a beginning or an end, but it doesn't have both. Some of the details in the middle don't belong there.
1 Huh?	The ideas don't go together. I can't tell what the writing is about.	The writing does not have a beginning. The writing does not have an end.

© NGSP & HB

Name _____   Date _____

Details Cluster

Complete the details cluster for your photo-essay.

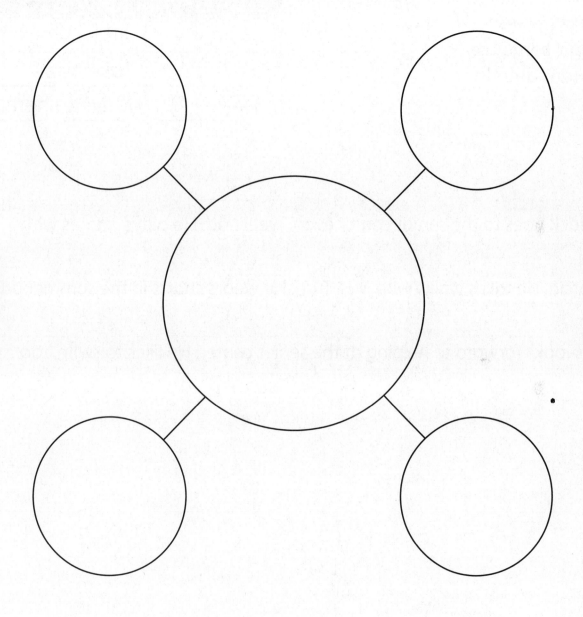

Writing Project

Revise

Use the Revising Marks to revise this paragraph. Look for:

- a topic sentence
- relevant details

Revising Marks	
∧	Add.
✐	Take out.
⬭⤴	Move to here.

Jack goes to the senior center every weekend. He plays games with

Mr. Garcia. He takes walks with Mrs. Tran. He wears shorts in the summer. Jack

always looks forward to helping at the senior center! He likes to swim, too.

Edit and Proofread

Use the Editing Marks to edit and proofread this paragraph. Look for:

- correct spelling of regular plural nouns
- correct form of irregular plural nouns
- capitalization of proper nouns

Editing Marks	
∧	Add.
℘	Take out.
⬯⌐	Move to here.
⬯	Check spelling.
≡	Capitalize.

Anna garcia is a very special person. She works in the

animal shelter on main Street. She takes care of all the dog and

cats. Sometimes she takes care of rabbits and mouses, too!

Every day she brushes the dogs. They give her lots of kisss.

Name _____ Date _____

Staying Alive

Make a concept map with the answers to the Big Question: What does it take to survive?

What do living things do to survive?

2.1

© NGSP & HB

Name _____   Date _____

The Nature Walk

Make a story map to tell about a nature walk.

Beginning:

How does the story start?

Middle:

What happens next in the story?

End:

How does the story end?

 Share your Beginning-Middle-End Chart with your a partner.

Grammar: Action Verbs

At the Park

Grammar Rules Action Verbs

An action verb tells what a person, animal, or thing does.

The boy <u>runs</u>.   His parents <u>talk</u>.

Add an –s to most action verbs to tell what one person, animal, or thing does.

Our dog <u>chases</u> squirrels.

Do not add –s to tell what two or more people, animals, or things do.

The squirrels <u>climb</u> the tree.

Write the correct form of the verb to complete each sentence. Then read the sentence to a partner.

1. see   The girl _____*sees*_____ a pair of robins.

2. build   The birds _____ a nest.

3. lay   The mother robin _____ three eggs.

4. open   The eggs _____ in two weeks.

5. feed   The parents _____ their hungry babies.

6. cheep   A hungry baby _____ .

7. swallow   The baby _____ a worm.

8. grow   The baby robins _____ quickly.

© NGSP & HB

Name _____ Date _____

Twilight Hunt

1

The Screech Owl's babies are hungry. It begins to hunt for food.

2

It looks for movements and listens for sounds. It sees many creatures, but it cannot catch them.

3

Finally, it catches a Luna Moth. A Great Horned Owl is watching the Screech Owl.

4

The Screech Owl hides in a tree. It waits. Then it takes the food home to its babies.

Name _____   Date _____

What Can I Do? What May I Find?

Grammar Rules Helping Verbs

Can, **may**, and **might** are helping verbs. Use them with **action verbs**.

> Mike **can swim** like a fish.
>
> He **may go** to the pool tomorrow.
>
> I **might swim** with him, too.

1. Can you hop like a katydid? Can you jump like a frog? Write about something you are able to do.

I _____

_____

2. Pretend you are walking in the woods. Write about something that is possible to see. Use the helping verb may.

I may _____

_____

3. Imagine you are an owl hunting for food. Write a sentence about what you might find.

I _____

_____

 Tell a partner which story event was your favorite and why.

© NGSP & HB

Name _____   Date _____

Twilight Hunt

Make a Beginning-Middle-End Chart to show the plot of "Twilight Hunt."

Beginning:
Screech Owl goes on a hunt. She must find food for her babies.

Middle:

End:

 Use your Beginning-Middle-End chart to tell your partner about "Twilight Hunt."

© NGSP & HB

Name _____ Date _____

Fluency: Expression

Expression is how you use your voice to express feelings to practice reading fluently with correct expression.

Twilight Hunt

Sensing danger, the Screech Owl swoops to land. 8

With feathers pulled tight, the 13

Screech Owl has disappeared. 17

So, the Great Horned Owl flies on. 24

Fluency: Expression

[B] ☐ Does not change read with feeling   [A] ☐ Reads with appropriate feeling for most content.

[I] ☐ Reads with some feeling, but does not match content   [AH] ☐ Read with appropriate feeling for all content.

Accuracy and Rate Formula

Use the formula to measure a reader's accuracy and rate while reading aloud.

$$\underline{\hspace{4cm}} - \underline{\hspace{4cm}} = \underline{\hspace{4cm}}$$

words attempted   number of errors   words corrected per
in one minute   minute (wcpm)

Name _____   Date _____

Hide and Seek

Complete this chart as you read "Hide and Seek."

K What I Know	W What I Want to Learn	L What I Learned	Q What I Still Want to Learn

 Share ideas with a partner. Tell which animal is your favorite and why.

Name _____ Date _____

Compare Genres

Compare a story and a science article.

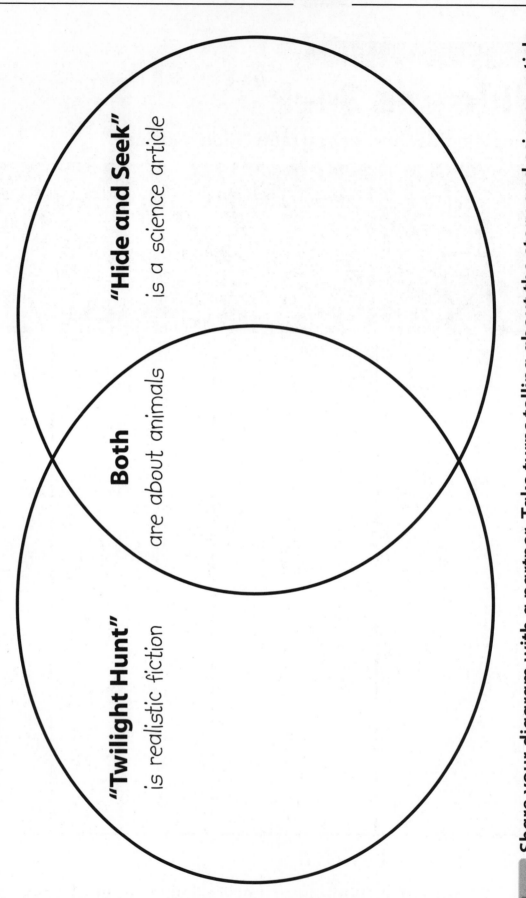

"Hide and Seek" is a science article

Both are about animals

"Twilight Hunt" is realistic fiction

Share your diagram with a partner. Take turns telling about the story and science article.

Name _____ Date _____

Roll a Verb

Grammar Rules Action and Helping Verbs

For Action Verbs

- Use **-s** at the end of an action verb if the subject is **he**, **she**, or **it**.
- Do not use **-s** for **I**, **you**, **we**, or **they**.

For Action Verbs with Helping Verbs

- A **helping verb** comes before the <u>main verb</u>.

Use a numbered game cube to play this game.

1. Roll the game cube. Find the helping verb that goes with the number.

2. Roll the game cube again. Find the action verb that goes with the number.

Helping Verbs	Action Verbs
1. do	1. look
2. does	2. escape
3. can	3. fly
4. might	4. run
5. do	5. search
6. can	6. hide

3. Say a sentence with the action verb and helping verb. The first player to use all 6 action verbs and helping verbs in sentences correctly wins.

© NGSP & HB

Name _____ Date _____

Creature Features

Compare animals and their features.

Features	Creature 1	Creature 2

 Tell a partner how the animals are alike.

2.11

Grammar: Verb *be*

Going to the Zoo

Grammar Rules Verb *be*		
Verbs should match what they are telling about.		
For yourself, use	**am**	I **am** a shark. I'm hungry!
For one other person or thing, use	**is**	A fish **is** my prey. It's tasty.
For one other person, yourself and others, or other people and things, use	**are**	My teeth **are** sharp. They **are** good for biting food. You **are** in trouble!

Write the correct form of the verb *be* to complete each sentence.

1. I _____am_____ happy!

2. We _____ at the zoo.

3. That elephant _____ very big.

4. The young elephants _____ cute.

5. The tiger _____ hungry.

6. You _____ too close to the cage!

 Read each sentence to a partner.

© NGSP & HB

Living Lights

1 Living things use light to survive. Some mushrooms use light to attract insects. The insects spread the mushroom spores. A spore is like a seed.

2 Animals use light to catch other animals. Glowworms use light to catch insects in their sticky threads. Then they eat the insects.

3 Insects use light to send messages. Fireflies flash lights to find each other.

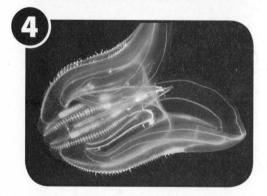

4 Ocean animals use light to escape from predators. Bioluminescent animals are hard to see in bright water.

© NGSP & HB

Grammar: Verb *have*

Sentence Building

1. Take turns with a partner.

2. Toss a marker onto the game board.

3. Make a sentence for the subject you land on. Use the correct form of *have*.

I	They	It
Animals	The insect	The scientist
We	You	Light

Living Lights

Make a chart to compare bioluminescent animals.

How It Uses Light	Animal
to attract prey	glowworm anglerfish
to send messages	
to hide	

 Use your comparison chart to tell a partner about the animals in "Living Lights."

© NGSP & HB

Fluency: Phrasing

Use this passage to practice reading fluently with correct phrasing.

Living Lights

Sometimes insects carry spores to new places.   7

Light attracts insects.   10

When they land on the glowing mushrooms,   17

some spores might stick to them.   23

When the insects leave, so do the spores!   31

Fluency: Phrasing

[B] ☐ Rarely pauses while reading the text.   [A] ☐ Frequently pauses at appropriate points in the text.

[I] ☐ Occasionally pauses while reading the text.   [AH] ☐ Consistently pauses at all appropriate points in the text.

Accuracy and Rate Formula

Use the formula below to measure a reader's accuracy and rate while reading aloud.

$$\underset{\substack{\text{words attempted} \\ \text{in one minute}}}{\underline{\hspace{3cm}}} - \underset{\text{number of errors}}{\underline{\hspace{3cm}}} = \underset{\substack{\text{words correct per minute} \\ \text{(wcpm)}}}{\underline{\hspace{3cm}}}$$

© NGSP & HB

Compare Genres

Use a comparison chart to compare "Living Lights" and "Clever Creatures."

Features	"Living Lights"	"Clever Creatures"
is about animals		
includes words that rhyme		
has facts		
has photographs		
has illustrations		

 Work with a partner. Read each feature and see if it is in "Living Lights" and "Clever Creatures." Make a check if you see the feature.

© NGSP & HB

Grammar: Verbs *be* and *have*

Insects at the Zoo

Grammar Rules Verbs *be* and *have*

Verbs should match who or what they are telling about.

For yourself, use	**am**	I **am** a scientist.
	have	I **have** work to do.
For one other person or thing, use	**is**	The Io moth **is** very clever.
	has	It **has** wings that look like big eyes.
For one other person, yourself and others, or other people and things, use	**are**	These wings **are** a clever trick.
	have	Many moths **have** features that keep them safe.

Choose the correct verb. Then read the sentence to a partner.

1. My teacher _____is_____ interested in all kinds of insects.

is/are

2. He _____ good news for our class.

has/have

3. We _____ on our way to the zoo on Friday!

is/are

4. The zoo _____ a special place to see insects.

has/have

5. I _____ excited about the trip to the zoo.

am/is

6. You _____ invited to come, too!

is/are

© NGSP & HB

Development of Ideas

	Is the writing interesting and unusual?	How well do you understand the ideas?
4 Wow!	• The writer has thought about the topic carefully. • The ideas are presented in a very interesting way.	• The ideas are supported with important details and examples. • The writing feels complete.
3 Ahh.	• The writer has thought about the topic. • The ideas are presented in an interesting way.	• Most of the ideas are supported with details and examples. • The writing feels mostly complete, but I still have some questions.
2 Hmm.	• The writer doesn't seem to have thought about the topic very much. • The writing is OK, but not very interesting.	• Details and examples are limited. • I have many questions about the information.
1 Huh?	• The writer doesn't seem to have thought about the topic at all. • The ideas are presented in a boring way.	• There aren't details to support the main idea. • The writing feels incomplete.

© NGSP & HB

Name _____ Date _____

Comparison Chart

Complete the comparison chart for your article.

My article is about _____ and _____.

Group:	Facts, Details, and Examples
	• •
	• •
	• •

Writing Project

Revise

Use the Revising Marks to revise this paragraph. Look for:

- a topic sentence
- relevant details

Revising Marks	
∧	Add.
℘	Take out.
⬭↷	Move to here.

I like tree frogs and moths. They can protect themselves.

Moths are brown like tree bark. Hungry birds can't see them.

Birds are very pretty. Tree frogs can blend into green leaves and

branches. They have tiny feet, too.

© NGSP & HB

Name _____ Date _____

Edit and Proofread

Use the Editing Marks to edit and proofread this paragraph. Look for:
- subject-verb agreement
- correct use of apostrophes in contractions
- correct spelling of compound words

Editing Marks	
∧	Add.
⅃	Take out.
⌒⌒	Move to here.
⌒	Delete space

Fish protect themselves in different ways. Minnows swims

in big schools. Bigger fish ca'nt catch them. Some fish hides in side

poisonous plants. Bigger fish do'nt wants to eat them. Some fish

are the same color as rocks and plants. They can blend into the

bacground. Fish is amazing!

Name _____   Date _____

Water for Everyone

Make a concept map with the answers to the Big Question: Where does water come from?

Where does water come from?

Where does water go?

3.1

© NGSP & HB

Name _____ Date _____

Problem and Solution

Fill out a problem-and-solution chart.

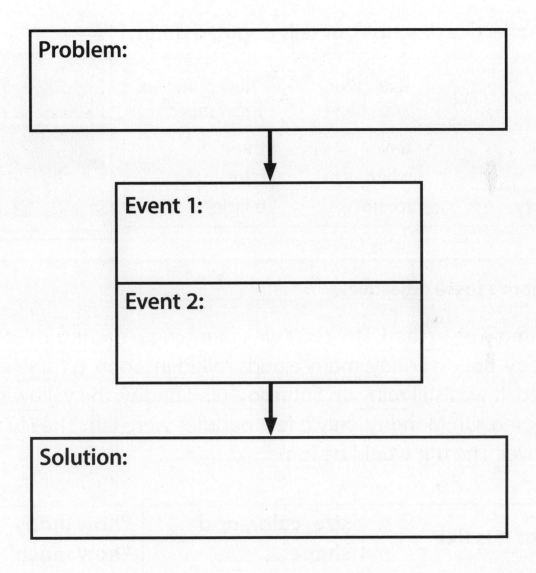

Problem:

Event 1:

Event 2:

Solution:

 Tell a partner about a problem you solved.

Grammar: Adjectives That Describe

A Rainy Weekend

Grammar Rules Adjectives

An adjective describes, or tells about, a noun.

what it is like	size, color, and shape	"how many" or "how much"
loud	tiny	three
icy	white	a lot
scary	round	a little

Categorize these adjectives.

Emma was <u>excited</u>. Her class was planning a <u>great</u> trip for Monday. But on Friday, <u>many</u> clouds rolled in. Soon, a <u>huge</u> storm started. It was still <u>rainy</u> on Saturday. On Sunday, the <u>yellow</u> sun appeared. On Monday, only <u>a few</u> puddles were left. The <u>icy</u> storm was over. The trip would be <u>fun</u>!

what it is like	size, color, and shape	"how many" or "how much"
excited		

Tell a partner about a storm you have seen. Use adjectives.

© NGSP & HB

Name _____ Date _____

Frog Brings Rain

1  Fire is moving to the First People's homes. Cardinal warns First Woman. First Man tells First Woman that Water will put out Fire.

2  First Woman makes a bottle and fills it with Water. Robin carries it to Fire. There isn't enough water to put Fire out. First Woman asks for help, but nobody will help her.

3  Finally, First Woman asks Frog to help. He soaks up Water in his coat. Then White Crane carries Frog over Fire. Water falls from Frog's coat as Rain. Water puts out Fire.

To this day, Frog lives in this swamp. He brings Rain with his song.

© NGSP & HB

Grammar: Adjectives and Articles

Animal Mix-Up

Play the Game

1. Choose a word from each column.

2. Act out the animal for your partner.

3. Your partner gets:
   - 1 point for guessing the animal
   - 1 point for guessing the adjective

4. Trade roles.

5. The partner with the most points wins.

Article	Adjective	Animal
a	angry	bear
an	brave	beaver
the	excited	crane
	friendly	fish
	huge	frog
	quiet	snail

© NGSP & HB

Vocabulary: Apply Word Knowledge

Vocabulary Bingo

1. Write one Key Word in each cloud.

2. Listen to the clues. Find the Key Word and use a marker to cover it.

3. Say "Bingo" when you have four markers in a row.

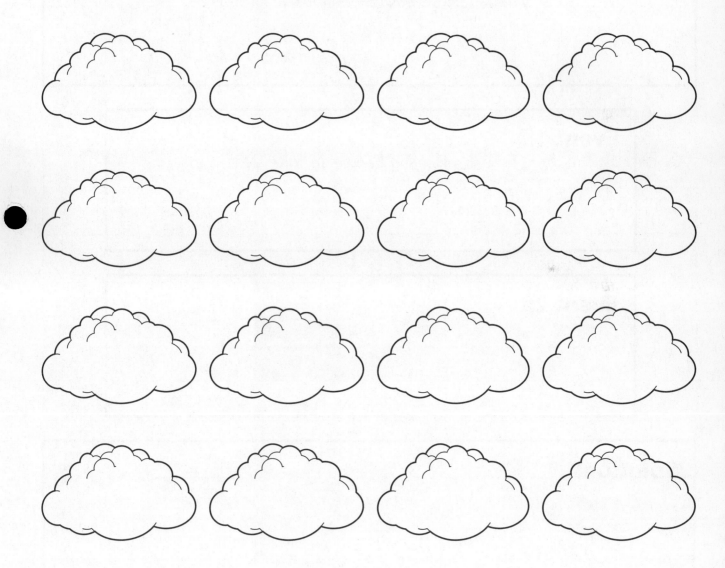

Name _____ Date _____

Frog Brings Rain

Use a problem-and-solution chart to tell about "Frog Brings Rain."

> **Problem:**
> First Woman needs Water to put out Fire.

↓

> **Event 1:**
> She asks Hunting People to take Water to Fire.

↓

> **Event 2:**

↓

> **Solution:**

 Use your chart to tell a partner how First Woman and Frog solve the problem.

© NGSP & HB

Name _____   Date _____

Fluency: Expression

Frog Brings Rain

Use this passage to practice reading fluently with correct expression.

On the east side, it fell as white rain. On the   11

west side, it was yellow rain.   17

Water put out Fire. Then Frog and Crane   25

returned home.   27

Expression

| B | ☐ Does not read with feeling. | | A | ☐ Reads with appropriate feeling for most content. |

| I | ☐ Reads with some feeling, but it does not match content. | | AH | ☐ Reads with appropriate feeling for all content. |

Accuracy and Rate Formula

Use the formula below to measure a reader's accuracy and rate while reading aloud.

$$\underline{\hspace{3cm}} - \underline{\hspace{3cm}} = \underline{\hspace{3cm}}$$

| words attempted in one minute | number of errors | words corrected per minute (wcpm) |

© NGSP & HB

Name _____ Date _____

Compare Explanations

Show how the two explanations for rain are different.

How Is Rain Made?	
Traditional Tale Explanation	**Science Experiment Explanation**
• Frog carries water.	• Warm, wet air rises.

 Ask a partner questions about the story and the science experiment.

© NGSP & HB

Name _____ Date _____

After the Storm

Grammar Rules Adjectives and Articles

Adjectives and articles can come before nouns.

An **adjective** can describe what a noun is like.	A **light** rain starts to fall. The raindrops feel **icy** and **cold**.
An **article** can tell which noun you mean.	**A** cloud fills up with water. Raindrops fall on **the** green hill. It is **an** amazing thing to see.

Add adjectives and articles.

The storm lasted for ___three___ days. Then the _____ sun rose. It dried up the _____ grass. _____ puddles started to disappear. Then we looked up into the _____ sky. There was _____ amazing rainbow. It looked _____ and _____. Soon the weather was _____ and _____ again.

 Tell a partner about weather you like. Use adjectives and articles.

Thinking Map: Cause-and-Effect Chart

Cause and Effect

Fill out a cause-and-effect chart to show what happened when you did something.

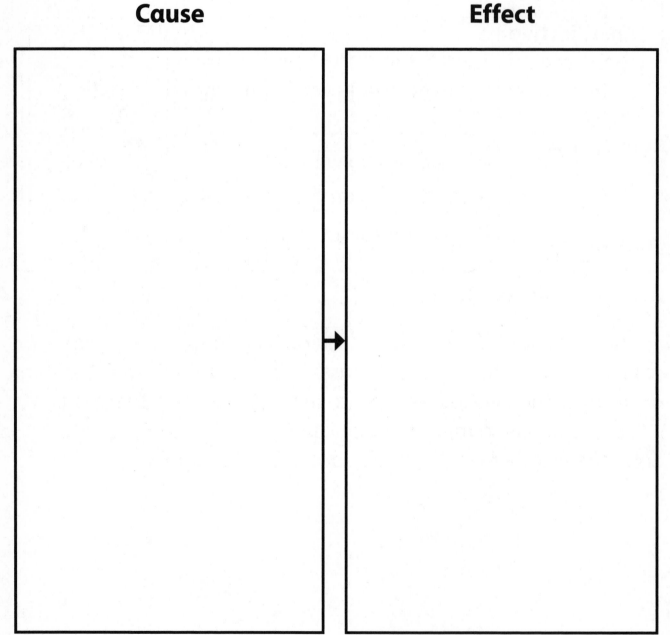

Cause   **Effect**

 Tell a partner about what happened and why.

© NGSP & HB

Grammar: Adverbs with -ly

Going to the Lake

Grammar Rules Adverbs with -ly

Adverbs tell about actions. Many **adverbs** tell how something happens. These adverbs usually end in **-ly**.

The sun rose **slowly**.

Anna got up **quickly**.

Read the adverbs in the box. Write the adverb that will correctly complete each sentence. Then read each sentence to a partner.

brightly	softly	loudly	proudly	quickly	safely

1. The sun shines _____*brightly*_____ in the sky.

2. "Are you ready to go?" Mom whispered _____.

3. "YES!" Anna yelled _____.

4. "I remembered to pack my life vest," Anna said _____.

5. "The vest will help me swim _____," Anna added.

6. Mom and Anna packed the car _____ and took off.

© NGSP & HB

Name _____   Date _____

PlayPumps Turning Work into Play

1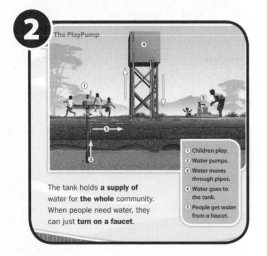

Everyone needs water to drink, cook, and clean. Some countries have a lot of clean water. In other countries, clean water is hard to find.

2

A new invention is bringing water to Africa. Children play on the PlayPump. As it spins, it pumps clean water from under the ground. The water goes into a water tank. The tank holds water for the community.

3

Now getting clean water is fast, easy, and fun. The pumps bring water to almost two million people.

© NGSP & HB

Grammar: Adverbs That Tell When

When Did It Happen?

Grammar Rules Adverbs That Tell When

Some **adverbs** tell when something happens.

> **Years ago** we got a water pump.
>
> **Last week** our water pump broke.
>
> **Then** we ran out of water.
>
> **Today** we fixed the pump.

Read the sentences. Circle the adverbs that tell when.

1. (Years ago) many people in Africa did not have water.

2. Then someone came up with the idea of PlayPumps.

3. Now PlayPumps help bring water to many towns.

4. Children often play and make the pumps work.

5. Many more people have water today.

Write a sentence about when you last drank some water. Remember to use an adverb that tells when. Share your sentence with a partner.

_____

_____

_____

© NGSP & HB

Name _____   Date _____

PlayPumps

Use a cause-and-effect chart to tell about "PlayPumps."

Cause	Effect
Kids ride on the PlayPump and turn the wheel.	

💬 **Use your chart to tell a partner about more causes and effects in "PlayPumps."**

© NGSP & HB

● **Fluency: Intonation**

PlayPumps

Intonation is how you raise and lower your voice. Use this passage to practice reading fluently with correct intonation.

PlayPumps are made in South Africa. Today,   7

there are more than 1,200 PlayPumps in five   15

African countries. They bring water to almost   22

two million people.   25

●

Fluency: Intonation

| B | ☐ Does not change pitch | | A | ☐ Changes pitch to match some of the content |
| I | ☐ Changes pitch, but does not match content | | AH | ☐ Changes pitch to match all the content |

Accuracy and Rate Formula

Use the formula below to measure a reader's accuracy and rate while reading aloud.

_____ – _____ = _____
words attempted   number of errors   words correct per minute
in one minute   (wcpm)

Name _____ Date _____

The Mighty Colorado

❶ What is the author's purpose for writing?

    ☐ to tell a story   **OR**   ☐ to give information

    ☐ to entertain

❷ What is your purpose for reading?

    ☐ for enjoyment   **OR**   ☐ for information

❸ What type of story are you going to read?

    ☐ fiction   **OR**   ☐ nonfiction

To read fiction:

- Identify the characters and settings.
- Think about what happens and when it happens.
- Use what you know to read new words.

To read nonfiction:

- Read more slowly.
- Identify facts about real people or events.
- Use maps, diagrams and photographs.
- Concentrate as you read.

Name _____   Date _____

Compare Information

Use a comparison chart to compare "PlayPumps" and "The Mighty Colorado."

How People Get Water	
"PlayPumps"	**"The Mighty Colorado"**
• Kids play.	

 Share your chart with a partner. Take turns asking questions about the information.

Grammar: Adverbs

Adverb Tic-Tac-Toe

1. **Play with a partner.**
2. **Player X chooses and reads the sentence. Player Y tells if the adverb tells how or when.**
3. **Player Y marks the square if the answer is correct.**
4. **Then players switch roles.**
5. **Keep taking turns to see if one player can get three marks in a row.**

The water stopped <u>yesterday</u>.	We <u>quickly</u> called the plumber.	The plumber arrived <u>soon</u>.
The plumber worked <u>carefully</u> to find the clog.	She <u>finally</u> found the clog.	<u>Then</u> she cleared it up.
<u>Slowly</u> the water began to flow.	We have plenty of water <u>today</u>.	We <u>gladly</u> fill our water jugs.

© NGSP & HB

Writing Project: Rubric

Voice and Style

	Does the writing sound real?	Do the words fit the purpose and audience?
4 Wow!	• The writing shows who the writer is. • The writer seems to be talking right to me.	• The writer uses words that really fit the purpose and audience.
3 Ahh.	• The writing shows who the writer is. • The writer seems to care about the ideas in the writing.	• The writer uses good words for the purpose and audience.
2 Hmm.	• It's hard to tell who the writer is. • The writer doesn't seem to be talking to me.	• The writer uses some words that fit the audience and purpose.
1 Huh?	• I can't tell who the writer is. • The writer doesn't seem to care.	• The words don't fit the purpose and audience.

Name _____   Date _____

Problem-and-Solution Chart

Complete the problem-and-solution chart for your folk tale.

Problem:

↓

Event 1:
Event 2:

↓

Solution:

© NGSP & HB

Revise

Use the Revising Marks to revise the paragraph. Look for:

- a clear description of the problem
- a unique voice
- precise words

Revising Marks	
∧	Add.
⟑	Take out.
⟲⟶	Move to here.

Ocean was sad. Ocean wanted friends. Everyone was scared

of Ocean. Ocean stopped making waves. A boy saw no waves.

He said, "Look!" Everyone went in Ocean.

Writing Project

Edit and Proofread

Use the Editing Marks to edit and proofread this paragraph. Look for:

- adjectives used correctly
- adverbs with **-ly**
- dialogue with quotation marks

Editing Marks	
∧	Add.
℘	Take out.
⟠⌐	Move to here.
⬭	Check spelling.
⸜⸝or ⸜	Insert quotation mark.

"I am lonely, said Ocean. Ocean's waves crashed loudly on the

sand. Ocean saw that the loudly waves scared people.

Sudden Ocean yelled, Wait! I have an idea!" Ocean made his

waves smaller and quieter. Then a little boy ran in and swam.

Other people went in, too.

"I am not lonely anymore," said Ocean happyly.

© NGSP & HB

Name _____   Date _____

Lend a Hand

Make a concept map with the answers to the Big Question: What are our responsibilities to each other?

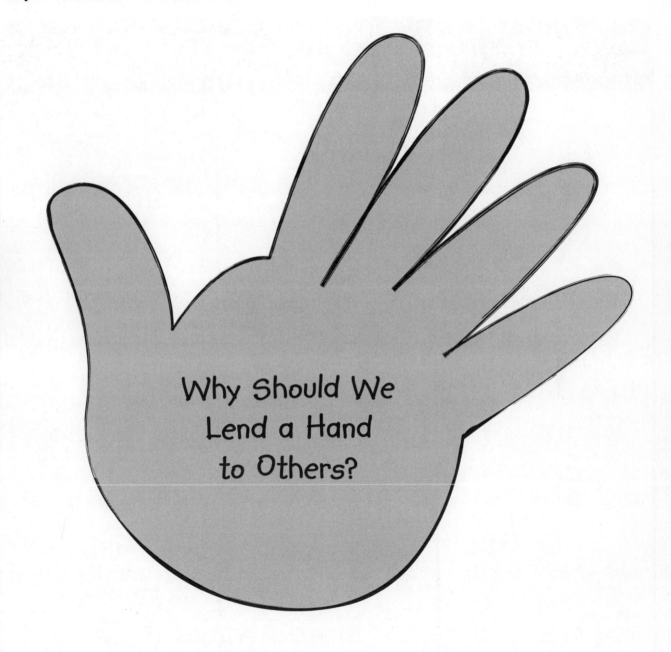

Why Should We
Lend a Hand
to Others?

Name _____ Date _____

Character Traits

Make a character map. Write about two characters you know.

Character	What the Character Does	What the Character Is Like

 Tell a partner which character was your favorite and why.

4.2

Name _____   Date _____

Helping Out

Grammar Rules Sentences: Word Order

A sentence has a naming part and a telling part.
The naming part usually comes before the telling part.

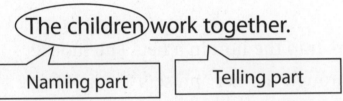

(The children) work together.

Naming part   Telling part

Circle the naming parts. Underline the telling parts.

1. (Enrique and Amy) start the meeting.

2. Everyone wants to clean up the school.

3. The teachers put trash bins around the yard.

4. The children pick up trash.

5. The school looks much better.

**Use the naming part of one sentence to make a new sentence.
Share your sentence with a partner.**

© NGSP & HB

Aesop's Fables

1

A mouse wakes a sleeping lion. He traps her under his paw. She begs him to let her go because she might be able to help him. The lion thinks it's a silly idea, but he lets her go.

2

Hunters trap the lion in a net. The mouse chews through the net and sets the lion free.
Moral: Great help can come from small friends.

3

Farmer Bean finds an eagle stuck in a mouse trap and sets him free.

4

Later, the farmer is eating beside a wall. The eagle takes his hat. He chases the eagle. It drops his hat. He goes back to the wall, but it has fallen down!
Moral: Help can come from unexpected places.

© NGSP & HB

Friends in Need

Grammar Rules Sentences

- Every sentence begins with a **capital letter**:
  F̲ables teach lessons about life.

- Every sentence ends with an end mark like a **period**:
  They are fun to read.̲

Write each sentence correctly. Use a capital letter and a period.

1. a farmer hears a cry in the barn

A farmer hears a cry in the barn. _____

2. he frees an eagle from a trap

_____

3. the eagle takes his hat

_____

4. a wall tumbles down

_____

5. the farmer is grateful

_____

 Write a complete sentence about one of the fables. Read it to your partner.

Name _____ Date _____

Aesop's Fables

Make a character map to tell about the characters in "Aesop's Fables."

Character	What the Character Does	What the Character Is Like
the lion	lets the mouse leave	generous
Farmer Bean		

 Use your character map to tell a partner about the characters in "Aesop's Fables."

4.6

© NGSP & HB

Aesop's Fables

Use this passage to practice reading with proper expression.

"Ah!" said the lion. "But you will make a tasty 10

snack." 11

"No, no!" the mouse pleaded. "What will my 19

babies do if you eat me?" 25

Expression

B ☐ Does not read with feeling.

A ☐ Reads with appropriate feeling for most content.

I ☐ Reads with some feeling, but does not match content.

AH ☐ Reads with appropriate feeling for all content.

Accuracy and Rate Formula

Use the formula to measure a reader's accuracy and rate while reading aloud.

_____ − _____ = _____

words attempted   number of errors   words correct per minute
in one minute   (wcpm)

Name _____ Date _____

Wisdom of the Ages

Use this reflection journal as you read the proverbs.

Page	Proverb	My Connection

 Tell a partner why a proverb has special meaning for you.

© NGSP & HB

Name _____   Date _____

Compare Settings and Plots

Use this comparison chart to compare the plots and settings of the two fables by Aesop.

Title	Setting	Plot
"The Lion and the Mouse"	takes place in the forest	
"The Farmer and the Eagle"		

  Share your comparison chart with a partner to talk about the fables.

Grammar: Complete Sentence

Build a Sentence Game

1. Play with a partner.

2. Toss a coin onto one of the sentence parts below.

3. Put it together with another sentence part to make a complete sentence.

4. Your partner takes a turn.

5. The player who makes the most complete sentences wins.

My friends	make good choices.
are thoughtful.	The teachers
My classmates	give to others.
help me study.	Mom and Dad
Our cousins	show respect.

© NGSP & HB

Thinking Map: Sequence Chain

Sequence

Fill out the sequence chain to show events in order.

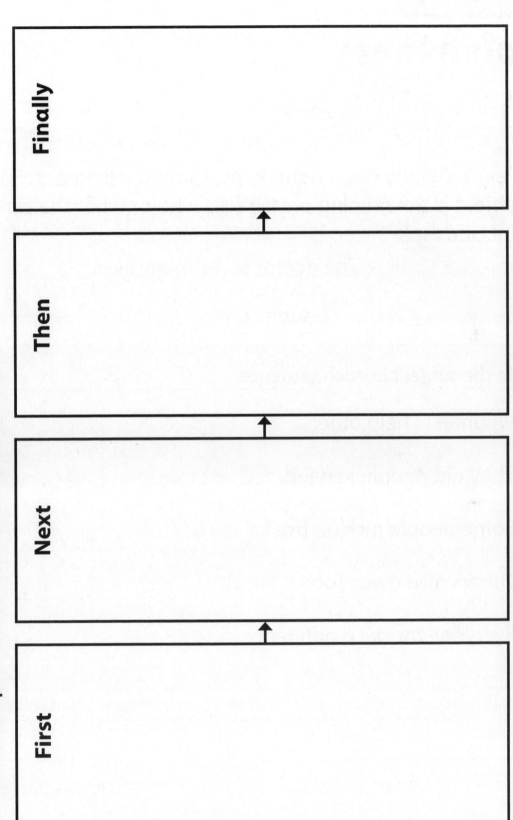

First	Next	Then	Finally

Use the sequence chain to tell the story to a partner.

Grammar: Subjects

Volunteers

Grammar Rules Subjects

Every sentence has a naming part and a telling part. The **subject** is the naming part. It tells who or what the sentence is about.

The <u>doctor</u> saves many lives.

subject

Circle the subject in each sentence.

1. Volunteers help others.

2. They aid people in need.

3. Some people pick up trash.

4. Others give away food.

5. Everyone makes a difference.

 Change the subject of a sentence to make a new sentence. Share your new sentence with a partner.

© NGSP & HB

Key Points Reading

Giving Back

William Allard is a photographer. While in Peru, he saw a boy on the side of a road. He was crying. A driver had killed his sheep. The boy was responsible for them. Allard took the boy's picture.

A magazine printed the picture. Readers sent money. An organization used the money to buy more sheep. It built a water pump for the boy's village. The rest of the money helped school children in Peru.

Allard's pictures have entertained people. This picture made someone's life better.

Name _____   Date _____

Happy to Help

Grammar Rules Predicates

Every sentence has a naming part and a telling part. The **predicate** is the telling part. It tells what the subject does.

The leader <u>decided on a plan</u>.
predicate

Underline the predicate in each sentence.

I <u>want to help others</u>. My family serves food to the poor. My generous friend comes to help. She gives money for food. Together, we feed many people that day. We both feel happy to help others.

 With a partner, change one of the predicates to make a new sentence.

© NGSP & HB

Reread and Retell: Sequence Chain

Giving Back

Fill out the sequence chain to show the order of events in "Giving Back."

First

William Allard sees a boy crying because his sheep have died.

↑

Next

↑

Then

↑

Finally

Tell a partner about the events in sequence.

Fluency: Phrasing

Giving Back

Use this passage to practice reading with proper expression.

When I got back to my hotel,   7

I thought a lot about Eduardo.   13

I thought about his broken sheep   19

and his tears.   22

I thought about his family.   27

I realized what it meant   32

to lose that many sheep.   37

The mountains of Peru   41

can be a hard place to live and work.   50

Phrasing

B ☐ Rarely pauses while reading the text.   A ☐ Frequently pauses at appropriate points in the text.

I ☐ Occasionally pauses while reading the text.   AH ☐ Consistently pauses at all appropriate points in the text.

Accuracy and Rate Formula

Use the formula to measure a reader's accuracy and rate while reading aloud.

$$\underline{\hspace{3cm}} - \underline{\hspace{3cm}} = \underline{\hspace{3cm}}$$

words attempted   number of errors   words correct per minute
in one minute   (wcpm)

Name _____   Date _____

Iraqi Children Get Wheelchairs—and Big Smiles

Record your thoughts about the news article in column 1. Then trade your dialogue journal with a partner. Write your response to what your partner wrote in column 2.

What I think	What do you think?
Pages _____ 	
Pages _____ 	
Pages _____ 	

Get together with your partner and compare your ideas and opinions.

© NGSP & HB

Name _____   Date _____

Compare Author's Purpose

Work with a partner to fill in the comparison chart.

Author's Purpose	William Allard	Carol Jordan and Arwa Damon
to persuade		
to inform		✓
to entertain		
to share experiences	✓	
to tell about other parts of the world		

Which selection did you like best? Share your opinion with a partner.

© NGSP & HB

Grammar: Subject-Verb Agreement

Do We Agree?

Grammar Rules Subject-Verb Agreement

Every sentence has two parts: the subject and the verb.
The subject and verb must agree.

The boy wait<u>s</u>.   **Parents** smile.

| one person | | more than one person |

1. Partner 1 points to a subject card.

2. Partner 2 points to a verb card.

3. If the subject and verb agree, cross out both cards.

4. Play until all the cards are crossed out.

Subject Cards			
Avi	Teresa	Mr. and Mrs. Mendez	You and I
He	She	They	We

Verb Cards			
wants	builds	helps	hopes
work	study	need	carry

Name _____   Date _____

Focus and Coherence

	How clearly does the writing present a topic?	How complete is the writing?
4 **Wow!**	The topic is clear. All of the questions and answers are about the topic.	The writing feels complete. The questions and answers are meaningful.
3 **Ahh.**	The topic is fairly clear. Most of the questions and answers are about the topic.	The writing feels mostly complete. The questions and answers add some meaning.
2 **Hmm.**	The topic is somewhat clear. At least one of the questions and answers is about the topic.	The writing feels somewhat complete. The questions and answers add little meaning.
1 **Huh?**	The topic is not clear. The questions and answers are not about the topic.	The writing feels incomplete. The questions and answers need work.

© NGSP & HB

Writing Project: Prewrite

Sequence Chain

Complete the Sequence Chain for your interview.

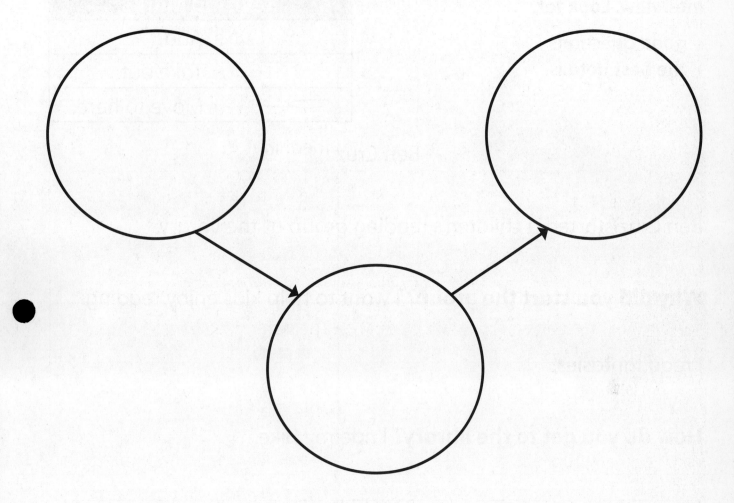

Revise

Use the Revising Marks to revise the interview. Look for:

- good questions
- the best details

Revising Marks	
^	Add.
℘	Take out.
⌢⟶	Move to here.

Ben Cruz

Ben Cruz started a children's reading group at the library.

Why did you start the group? I want to help kids enjoy reading.

I read fantasies.

How do you get to the library? I ride my bike.

How did you start the group? I told the librarian I could read on

Saturdays. She liked my plan. She helped me start the group.

When I'm done, I go play basketball.

Name _____   Date _____

Edit and Proofread

Use the Editing Marks to edit and
proofread the interview. Look for:

- complete sentences
- question marks
- a prefix

Editing Marks	
^	Add.
ϑ	Take out.
⬯⟋	Move to here.
⬯	Check spelling.

Isabel Vega

Isabel Vega walks her neighbor's dog, Mack.

Why did you start walking dogs? My neighbor broke her leg

because of a mistep. She can't walk her dog Mack.

How often do you walk her dog I walk her dog every morning.

Do you enjoys walking Mack? Yes, Mack is fun. He wags his

tail a lot.

Name _____ Date _____

Everything Changes

Make a concept map with the answers to the Big Question: Why is nature always changing?

Name _____ Date _____

My Favorite Story

Make a theme chart to tell the details about a favorite story.

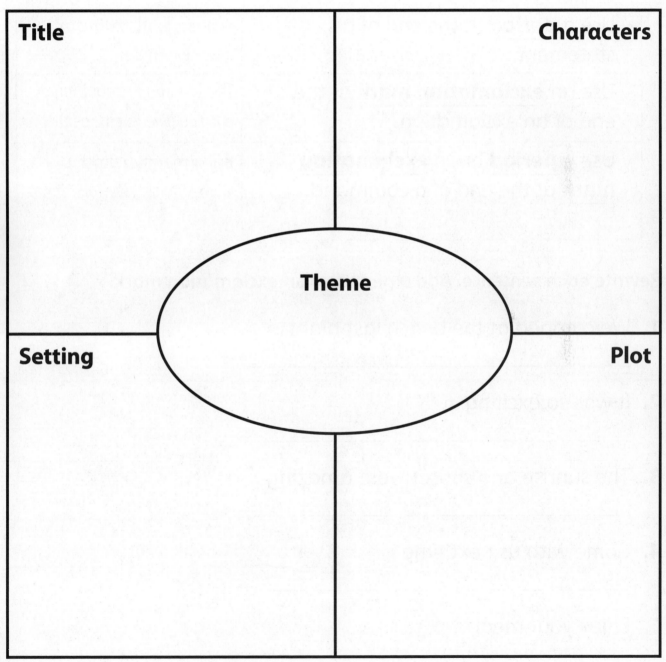

Title

Characters

Theme

Setting

Plot

💬 **Work with a partner to find the theme of your story.**

Name _____   Date _____

A Glorious Trip!

Grammar Rules Kinds of Sentences

• Use a **period** at the end of a statement.	Sunrise is at 6:00 a.m. this morning.
• Use an **exclamation mark** at the end of an exclamation.	It's the most beautiful sunrise I've ever seen!
• Use a **period** or an **exclamation mark** at the end of a command.	Bring me my camera. Come quickly before it's gone!

Rewrite each sentence. Add a period or an exclamation mark.

1. We camped at the beach last night

_____

2. It was so exciting

_____

3. The sunrise and sunset were amazing

_____

4. Come with us next time

_____

5. Enjoy your meal

_____

 Read your sentences to a partner. Use expression as you read exclamations and commands.

© NGSP & HB

Key Points Reading

When the Wind Stops

1  A boy wonders why the day ends. His mother tells him that it is so a new night can begin. A new day begins in another place. She tells the boy nothing ever ends.

2  The boy wonders where the wind goes. His mother tells him it blows away to make the trees dance somewhere else. She tells him after a storm the rain goes back to the clouds.

3  The mother tells the boy that the end of autumn is the beginning of winter. The end of winter is the beginning of spring.

4  The boy learns that nature goes on and on. Nothing ever ends.

Name _____   Date _____

Is It OK to be Negative?

Grammar Rules Kinds of Sentences

A question asks something. It ends with a **question mark**.

Is that your shadow**?**

A negative sentence uses a negative word, like **not**.

It usually ends with a **period**.

That is **not** my shadow**.**

For each sentence, underline the end punctuation. Then circle what type of sentence it is.

1. When does the moon appear? (negative sentence/ question)

2. It does not appear during the day. (negative sentence/ question)

3. Can you see the moon at night? (negative sentence/ question)

4. We will not miss it. (negative sentence/ question)

5. Do you want to learn more about the moon? (negative sentence/question)

 Tell a partner about the moon. Include one question and one negative sentence.

© NGSP & HB

Name _____ Date _____

When the Wind Stops

Use clues from the story to figure out the theme.

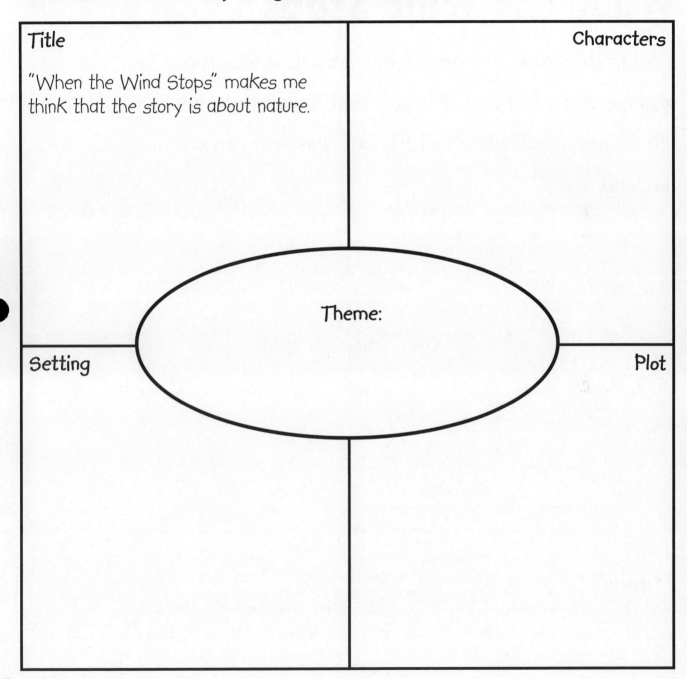

Title

"When the Wind Stops" makes me think that the story is about nature.

Characters

Theme:

Setting

Plot

 Share your clues and theme with a partner.

Name _____   Date _____

Use this passage to practice reading with proper expression.

When the Wind Stops

The bright sun had shone all day, and now the day   11

was coming to an end. The sun sank lower into the   22

glowing pink clouds. The little boy was sorry to see the   33

day end.   35

Expression

| B | ☐ Does not read with feeling | A | ☐ Reads with appropriate feeling for most content |

| I | ☐ Reads with some feeling, but does not match content | AH | ☐ Reads with appropriate feeling for all content |

Accuracy and Rate Formula

Use the formula to measure a reader's accuracy and rate while reading aloud.

_____ – _____ = _____

words attempted   number of errors   words correct per minute
in one minute   (wcpm)

© NGSP & HB

Day and Night

Record your ideas as you read "Day and Night."

What I Know	What I Want to Learn	What I Learned	Questions I Still Have

💬 **Tell a partner a fact you learned about night and day. Then write questions you still have in column 4.**

Name _____   Date _____

Compare Author's Purpose

Show why Charlotte Zolotow wrote "When the Wind Stops." Compare this to why Glen Phelan wrote "Day and Night."

Charlotte Zolotow	Glen Phelan
• to tell about how nature changes	• to tell about changes in nature

 Tell a partner which selection you liked better. Explain your favorite author's purpose for writing.

5.9

© NGSP & HB

Build a Sentence

1. Play with a partner.

2. Use the words below to build sentences. Write a question, a statement, a command, and an exclamation.

3. Begin with a capital letter. Add an end mark.

4. The player who first writes all four types of sentences correctly wins.

Is/is	night	beautiful
The/the	Do/do	star
your	see	shadow
Come/come	get	you
Are/are	book	That/that

_____

_____

_____

_____

Name _____   Date _____

Compare and Contrast

Complete the comparison chart below.

Picture Cards	How They Are Alike	How They Are Different
Picture Card 1: _____		
Picture Card 2: _____		

 Share your chart with a partner. Tell how your picture cards are alike and different.

© NGSP & HB

Name _____   Date _____

Grammar: Yes/No Questions

The Seasons

Grammar Rules Yes/No Questions

- Some questions have *Yes* or *No* answers. They start with a verb like *Is*, *Are*, *Do*, and *Does*. They end with a question mark (?).

Question	Answer
Are you cold?	Yes, I am cold.
Do you like snow?	No, I do not like snow.

Write an answer to each the question that says "yes" or "no."

1. Is winter a season?

_____

2. Do leaves fall in spring?

_____

3. Are there four seasons?

_____

4. Does it snow in summer?

_____

 Write your own question and have a partner answer it.

Key Points Reading

What Makes the Seasons?

1 Spring melts the snow. It brings rain and leaves begin to bud. Seeds sprout and grow. But spring cannot stay. It leaves on a summer day.

2 Summer brings the growing season. Flowers bloom and trees are green. The days are long, warm, and sunny.

3 When the summer ends, autumn days begin. Cold winds blow. The green leaves change colors and fall from the trees.

4 Winter brings snow. Everything sleeps. Trees and seeds rest. Animals hibernate. The seasons change because of Earth's yearly trip around the sun. When it is summer in one part of the world, it is winter in another.

© NGSP & HB

Grammar: Questions

Question Word Rivet

Grammar Rules Questions

Questions that ask for more information often start with *Who, What, Where, Why, When,* or *How.*

Who asks about a person.	*Why* asks for a reason.
What asks about a thing.	*When* asks about a time.
Where asks about a place.	*How* asks how things happen.

Each sentence needs a question word. Spell the question word that belongs with each sentence by filling in the blanks. Work with a partner to see who can complete the word first.

1. __ h __ tells you about weather in your city?

2. W __ __ did it snow early this year?

3. __ __ w does a thermometer work?

4. __ __ e __ will spring begin?

5. W __ __ __ happens when ice melts?

6. __ h __ __ __ is the hottest place on Earth?

5.14

Unit 5 | Everything Changes

Name _____   Date _____

What Makes the Seasons?

Complete the comparison chart below. Show how the seasons are alike and different.

	Spring	Summer	Fall	Winter
Leaves	sprout			
Raindrops	fall			
Snow	melts			
Days	get longer			

 Use the information from the chart to tell your partner how the seasons are alike and different.

© NGSP & HB

Fluency: Intonation

Use this passage to practice reading with proper intonation.

What Makes the Seasons?

Winter is a time for sleep.	6
Trees are resting. Seeds will keep.	12
Many creatures sleep and wait.	17
Winter's time to hibernate.	21
But what controls the season's change?	27
And what makes weather rearrange?	32
Earth's yearly trip around the sun	38
affects the seasons one by one.	44

Intonation

B ☐ Does not vary intonation or use end marks to determine whether voice should rise or fall during reading	**A** ☐ Varies intonation; usually uses end marks (questions marks and periods) to determine whether voice should rise or fall during reading
I ☐ Sometimes varies intonation, using end marks (questions marks and periods) to determine whether voice should rise or fall during reading	**AH** ☐ Varies intonation; always uses end marks to determine whether voice should rise or fall during reading

Accuracy and Rate Formula

Use the formula to measure a reader's accuracy and rate while reading aloud.

$$\underline{\hspace{3cm}} - \underline{\hspace{3cm}} = \underline{\hspace{3cm}}$$

words attempted in one minute	number of errors	words correct per minute (wcpm)

Name _____   Date _____

A Winter Wonder

Make fact cards about frogs. Write the topic, state a fact, and draw a picture on each card.

That's Amazing!

Fact Card 1

An amazing fact about _____

is _____

_____

_____ .

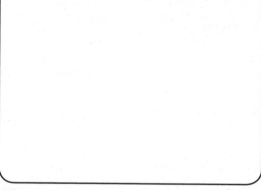

Picture

That's Amazing!

Fact Card 2

An amazing fact about _____

is _____

_____

_____ .

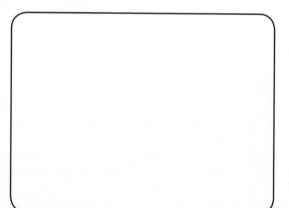

Picture

 Share your cards with a partner and compare facts.

© NGSP & HB

© NGSP & HB

Compare Genres: Venn Diagram

Compare Genres

Use the Venn diagram to tell how "What Makes the Seasons?" and "A Winter Wonder" are alike and different.

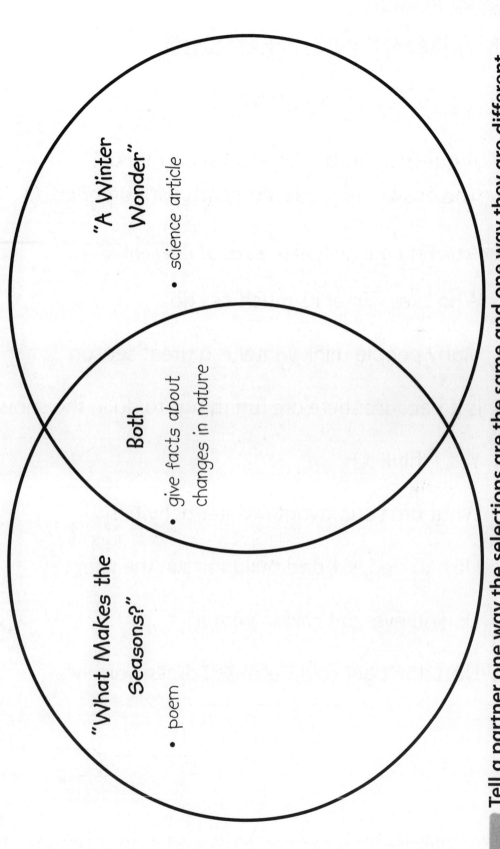

"A Winter Wonder"

• science article

Both

• give facts about changes in nature

"What Makes the Seasons?"

• poem

Tell a partner one way the selections are the same and one way they are different.

Name _____ Date _____

Grammar: Questions

Wonderful Winter

Grammar Rules Questions

- A question ends with a question mark. (?)
- The answer to a question ends with a period. (.)

Add correct punctuation to each of the sentences.

1. Who likes winter as much as I do

2. Many people think winter is a great season

3. Is it because there are fun things to do in the snow

4. Yes, I think it is

5. What are your favorite winter activities

6. I like to sled, ski, and build forts in the snow

7. Do you ever get cold in winter

8. No, I don't get cold because I dress warmly

 Work with a partner to ask and answer two questions about seasons.

For use with TE p. T325a   **5.19**   Unit 5 | Everything Changes

Name _____   Date _____

Organization

	Is the Writing Organized?	Does the Writing Flow?
4 Wow!	The writing is very well-organized. It fits the writer's purpose.	The writing is very smooth. Each idea flows into the next one.
3 Ahh.	The writing is organized. It fits the writer's purpose.	The writing is pretty smooth. There are only a few places where it jumps around.
2 Hmm.	The writing is organized, but it doesn't fit the writer's purpose.	The writing jumps from one idea to another idea, but I can follow it a little.
1 Huh?	The writing is not organized. Maybe the writer forgot to plan.	I can't tell what the writer wants to say.

Name _____   Date _____

Comparison Chart

Complete the chart for your comparison.

	Season: _____	Season: _____
Temperature		
Weather		
Sports		
_____		
_____		

5.21

© NGSP & HB

Writing Project

Revise

Use the Revising Marks to revise the paragraph. Look for:

- well organized ideas
- words that show comparisons
- correct spelling
- capitalization

Revising Marks	
∧	Add.
⌿	Take out.
⌒⟶∧	Move to here.

Winter and Summer

Winter and summer are my favorite seasons.

I like the hot weather in summer. I can swim at the beach. I can't swim in the winter. I can wear sandals and shorts. In winter, I need warm clothes.

The cold weather in winter lets me do winter activities. I love to ski and ice skate. Both winter and summer are fun. It's also fun to build a snowman.

Writing Project

Edit and Proofread

Use the Editing Marks to edit and
proofread the comparison. Look for:

- spellings with *ie* or *ei*
- different kinds of sentences and
  their punctuation
- apostrophes

Editing Marks	
∧	Add.
ᵧ	Take out.
⬭↰	Move to here.
⬭	Check spelling.
⊙	Insert period.
∧?	Insert question mark.

Weather Opposites

I live in Colorado. Summer and winter are very different here.

In the summer, the weather is hot, and I love hot weather? I go to
the lake with my freinds. We play volleyball and swim. We have fun
during summer?

Winter is very different. It can get very cold. If the temperature
gets in the 30's, we think it's warm. Why do I love winter! The snow is
pretty. My nieghbors' house has a warm fireplace. When my family
visits them, we drink hot cocoa at my friends house.

Winter and summer are very different, but I like them both.

Move to Colorado. Youll see what I mean.

Unit Concept Map

Better Together

Make a concept map with the answers to the Big Question: Why do people work together?

What happens when people work together?

Name _____ Date _____

Story Elements

Use a story map to tell about the characters, setting, and plot of a story.

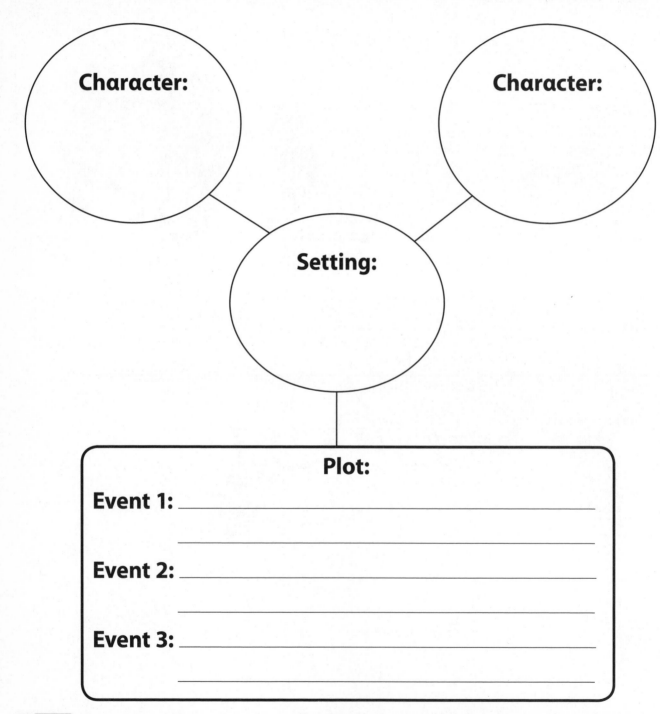

Character:

Character:

Setting:

Plot:

Event 1: _____

_____

Event 2: _____

_____

Event 3: _____

_____

Use your story map to tell a partner a story about being part of a team.

© NGSP & HB

Name _____ Date _____

We Care and Share!

Grammar Rules Subject Pronouns

Pronouns take the place of nouns. Use these subject pronouns to tell who or what does the action.

Example: Ernesto and I like to work. <u>We</u> work together.

One	More Than One
I	we
you	you
he, she, it	they

Write the correct pronoun to complete each sentence.

1. Jon likes to help. _____ helps his mom with the dishes.

2. Kate and Sanjay like to give. _____ give clothes to a shelter.

3. The truck picks up the clothes. _____ is a big truck.

4. Toby, Jill, and I like to share. _____ share our toys with one another.

5. Maya likes teamwork. _____ works best with others.

 Write your own sentence using a subject pronoun. Share your sentence with a partner.

Domino Soup

1 Luz wants to make a welcome dinner for the new neighbors. She thinks everyone can share a little food. But no one wants to share.

2 Luz has an idea. She asks Abuelo for a domino. She make Domino Soup. Everyone watches Luz make the soup.

3 Luz cooks the domino. She says it smells good. No one else can smell anything. Luz wants an onion to make the soup smell better. The grocer gets one. Soon, everyone is bringing things.

4 The new neighbors smell the soup. They knock at the door. Luz and her friends invite them to have some soup. They say the neighborhood is very kind-hearted. The neighbors all agree.

© NGSP & HB

Grammar: Object Pronouns

Soup for Us

Grammar Rules Object Pronouns

Pronouns take the place of nouns. Use object pronouns after action words or after words like *at, with, for, to,* or *of.*

Example: I want to make soup for **the neighbors**. I cook for **them**.

One	More Than One
me	us
you	you
him, her, it	them

Circle the object pronoun that takes the place of the noun.

1. Luz gets a **pot** and places it on the stove.

2. The butcher sees **Luz** and asks her if the soup needs chicken.

3. A neighbor brings **potatoes** and adds them to the pot.

4. Luz likes to cook for **Abuelo**. Luz gives some soup to him.

5. **My friend and I** see the baker. The baker shares his bread with us.

 Use an object pronoun in a new sentence. Then read your sentence to a partner.

© NGSP & HB

Name _____   Date _____

Domino Soup

Make a story map for "Domino Soup."

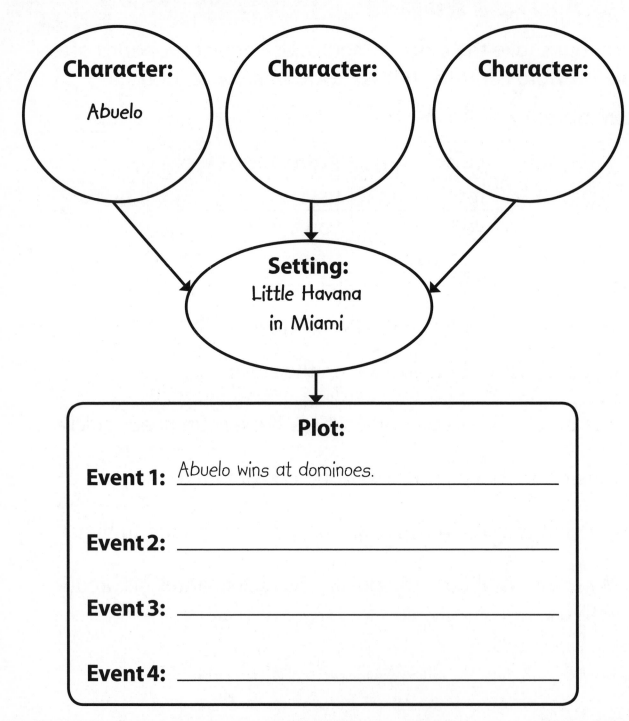

Character:
Abuelo

Character:

Character:

Setting:
Little Havana
in Miami

Plot:

Event 1: Abuelo wins at dominoes. _____

Event 2: _____

Event 3: _____

Event 4: _____

 Share your story map with a partner. Compare the story elements you found for "Domino Soup."

© NGSP & HB

Fluency: Expression

**Use this passage to practice reading with proper expression.
Do not read the character names.**

Domino Soup

BAKER	I hear there's a new family	6
	moving in next week.	10
NEIGHBOR 1:	I have a great idea!	15
	We should welcome them to the neighborhood	22
	with a big feast!	26
NEIGHBOR 2:	I'll bring the domino!	30

Expression

B ☐ Does not read with feeling.   A ☐ Reads with appropriate feeling for most content.

I ☐ Reads with some feeling, but does not match content.   AH ☐ Reads with appropriate feeling for all content.

Accuracy and Rate Formula

Use the formula to measure a reader's accuracy and rate while reading aloud.

$$\underline{\hspace{3cm}} - \underline{\hspace{3cm}} = \underline{\hspace{3cm}}$$

| words attempted in one minute | number of errors | words correct per minute (wcpm) |

NGSP & HB

Name _____ Date _____

Stone Soup

Complete this journal with a partner as you read "Stone Soup." Write your ideas in column 1. Have your partner write ideas in column 2.

What I think	What do you think?
Page _____ _____ _____ _____	_____ _____ _____ _____
Page _____ _____ _____ _____	_____ _____ _____ _____
Page _____ _____ _____ _____	_____ _____ _____ _____

Talk with your partner about how your opinions are the same and different.

© NGSP & HB

Name _____   Date _____

Compare Two Versions of the Same Story

Use the comparison chart to show how "Domino Soup" and "Stone Soup" are alike and different.

	"Domino Soup"	**"Stone Soup"**
Type of Story	play	song
Characters		
Setting		
Plot		

 Tell a partner how the two versions of the story are the same and different.

Name _____   Date _____

The Pronoun Game

1. Play with a partner.
2. Spin the spinner.
3. Name a pronoun to replace the words in the space.
4. Say a sentence using the pronoun.
5. Color in the space.
6. Play until all the spaces are colored in.

Make a Spinner

1. Put a paper clip ⊂⊐ in the center of the circle.

2. Hold one end of the paper clip with a pencil.

3. Spin the paper clip around the pencil.

one boy

one girl

yourself

one object

two or more people

you and a friend

© NGSP & HB

Name _____   Date _____

Main Idea

Make a main idea diagram to tell about a time you worked with someone to reach a goal.

Detail	**Detail**

Main Idea

 Share your main idea diagram with a partner.

© NGSP & HB

Name _____ Date _____

Our Class Project

Grammar Rules Possessive Adjectives

- A **possessive adjective** always comes before a noun. It tells who or what owns something.

  Example: We care about <u>our</u> education.

Singular	Plural
my	our
your	your
his, her, its	their

Write the possessive adjective that completes each sentence. Then circle the noun it describes.

1. This project belongs to all of you. This is __your__ project.

2. This dream belongs to me. This is _____ dream.

3. This is the boy's plan. This is _____ plan.

4. This is the project's result. This is _____ result.

5. These are the students' skills. These are _____ skills.

6. My classmates and I have these goals. These are _____ goals.

 Use a possessive adjective in a sentence about something that belongs to one or more people in your class. Share your sentence with a partner.

6.12

© NGSP & HB

Name _____ Date _____

In a Mountain Community

1 Chungba is a village in Tibet. People there are herders or farmers. Very few children went to school. The Rabgey family wanted a school for them.

2 The Rabgeys asked the community to help. They raised money. The people in the community helped build the school.

3 The children learn many subjects. They also care for the earth. They grow their own vegetables. They keep their village clean.

4 Chungba now has a middle school, too. The Rabgeys did not build the schools alone. Many volunteers worked together. They made the dream come true.

© NGSP & HB

Grammar: Possessive Pronouns

Our Class Fundraiser

Grammar Rules Possessive Pronouns

- A **possessive pronoun** shows ownership.
- Possessive pronouns do not come before nouns. They stand alone.

  Example: That plan is <u>theirs</u>.

Singular	Plural
mine	ours
yours	yours
his, hers	theirs

Fill in the blank with the correct possessive pronoun.

1. This idea for a fundraiser belongs to us. The idea is <u>ours</u>.

2. This is her plan for the event. This plan is _____.

3. You and Mario have the lists of what we will need. These lists are _____.

4. This chart belongs to him. This chart is _____.

5. These are their tools. These tools are _____.

6. This is my hope for the event. This hope is _____.

7. This is your opportunity. This opportunity is _____.

> **Write a sentence that uses a possessive pronoun to tell who owns or has something. Share the sentence with a partner.**

Vocabulary: Apply Word Knowledge

Vocabulary Bingo

1. **Write one Key Word in each school.**
2. **Listen to the clues. Find the Key Word and color it in.**
3. **Say "Bingo" when you have four markers in a row.**

Key Words	
dream	plan
education	project
join	result
opportunity	skill
organize	success

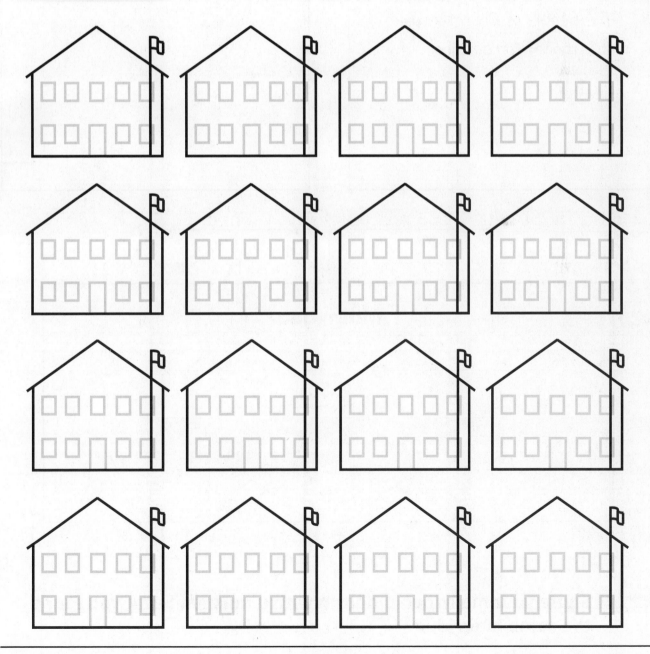

© NGSP & HB

In a Mountain Community

Make a main idea diagram for "In a Mountain Community."

Detail	**Detail**
The people of Chungba raise money for a school.	

Main Idea

 Share your main idea diagram with a partner. See if you found the same main idea.

© NGSP & HB

Fluency: Phrasing

In a Mountain Community

Use this passage to practice reading with proper phrasing.

A Bright Future	3
The Rabgeys and Machik	7
worked with many others	11
to build the schools.	15
Volunteers from Chungba	18
and around the world helped.	23
They all worked hard	27
to make	29
the Chungba people's dream	33
come true.	35

Phrasing

[B] ☐ Rarely pauses while reading the text   [A] ☐ Frequently pauses at appropriate points in the text

[I] ☐ Occasionally pauses while reading the text   [AH] ☐ Consistently pauses at all appropriate points in the text

Accuracy and Rate Formula

Use the formula to measure a reader's accuracy and rate while reading aloud.

_____ − _____ = _____
  words attempted   number of errors   words correct per minute
    in one minute   (wcpm)

© NGSP & HB

Name _____   Date _____

Compare Texts

Use the comparison chart to show how "In a Mountain Community" and "Mi Barrio" are alike and different.

	"In a Mountain Community"	"Mi Barrio"
It is in an urban community.		✓
It is in a rural community.	✓	
The community members help each other.		
The children help their community, too.		
The selection is illustrated with photographs.		
It is a true story.		

 Compare your chart with a partner's. See if you found the same information.

© NGSP & HB

Grammar: Possessive Pronouns

Possessive Pronoun Concentration

1. Play with 2 or 3 people. Copy all the words below onto separate cards.
2. Mix the cards up and put them face down.
3. Turn over two cards. If the possessive pronoun card matches the noun card, keep both cards. If the two cards do not match, turn them face down again in the same place.
4. The player with the most cards at the end wins.

Nouns			
Lee and Ana's notes	Our project	Lupe's and your plans	Lilu's marker
My goals	Your skill	Jackson's paper	

Possessive Pronouns			
Mine	Yours	Ours	Theirs
His	Hers	Yours	

Use three of the nouns above. Tell a partner something about you.

© NGSP & HB

Organization

	Is the Whole Thing Organized?	Does the Writing Flow?
4 Wow!	• The writing is very well-organized. • It fits the writer's purpose.	• The writing is very smooth. Each idea flows into the next one.
3 Ahh.	• The writing is pretty organized in a few places, but it doesn't fit the writer's purpose.	• The writing is pretty smooth. There are only a few places where it jumps around.
2 Hmm.	• The writing is pretty organized, but it doesn't fit the writer's purpose.	• The writing jumps from one idea to another, but sometimes I can follow it.
1 Huh?	• The writing is not organized. • Maybe the writer forgot to use a story map to plan.	• I can't tell what the writer wants to say.

© NGSP & HB

Name _____   Date _____

Story Map

Complete the story map for your story.

Characters		Setting

Beginning

Middle

End

© NGSP & HB

Writing Project

Revise

Use the Revising Marks to revise the paragraph. Look for:
- character and setting descriptions
- missing details

Revising Marks	
^	Add.
৵	Take out.
⌄⌄	Insert quotation marks.
₱	Insert new paragraph.

Show Time

Tina looks at the kitchen sink. There are many dishes.

"It's your turn to do the dishes," says Tina's dad.

The movie starts in fifteen minutes. There are too many dishes!

Tina asks her big sister to help. "I will wash the dishes if you will dry

them. Then I will help you do dishes tomorrow."

Tina rushes next door to her friend's house. At her friend's, she sits

down to watch the movie.

© NGSP & HB

Writing Project

Edit and Proofread

Use the Revising Marks to edit and proofread this story. Look for:

- spelling of they're/their/there; its/it's; your/you're
- pronoun agreement
- end punctuation

Editing Marks	
∧	Add.
℘	Take out.
⊙	Insert period.
？	Insert question mark.
！	Insert exclamation point.
∧	Insert comma.
∨	Insert apostrophe.

A Clever Cat Trick

"Its time to take your cat to the vet, " Gabby's mom said. "Put

Buddy in their pet carrier."

Gabby looked everywhere for my cat. "Buddy! Where are you."

Gabby found Buddy hiding under the bed. "How will I get him out?"

Her had an idea.

Buddy loves cheese? Gabby made a cheese trail from the bed

into the pet carrier Slowly Buddy came out. He ate all the cheese

until he was inside the carrier.

Now there ready to take Buddy for his checkup at the vet.

Unit Concept Map

Best Buddies

Make a concept map with the answers to the Big Question: How do living things depend on each other?

Ways that living things depend on one another

Name _____   Date _____

Characters' Motives

Make a character map for the animal in your story.

Character	What the Character Does	Why the Character Does It

**Tell a partner your story. Then share your character map.
Talk about the character's motives.**

Grammar: Regular Past Tense Verbs

Food Chains

Grammar Rules Regular Past Tense Verbs

Use the past tense to tell about an action that has already happened. Add *-ed* to most verbs when you talk about a past action.

| jump | + | ed | = | jumped |

| wish | + | ed | = | wished |

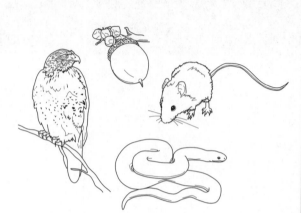

Change the verb in the box to the past tense. Say it. Then say the sentence and add the past tense verb.

1. chew The mouse _____ on an acorn.

2. want A snake _____ to catch the mouse.

3. hunt A hawk _____ the snake.

4. munch A rabbit _____ on the grass.

5. look A hawk _____ at the rabbit.

6. leap The rabbit _____ away from the hawk.

💬 **Choose a verb from one of the boxes and make a new sentence. Have a partner change the verb to make the sentence past tense.**

7.3

© NGSP & HB

Name _____   Date _____

Go to Sleep, Gecko!

1

Gecko wakes Elephant in the middle of the night. He can't sleep. The fireflies are blinking their lights around his house. He wants Elephant to make them stop.

2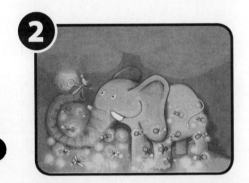

The fireflies tell Elephant that they blink their lights to keep people safe. People can fall into the holes Rain makes in the road.

3

Gecko wakes Elephant up again. Elephant says Gecko must live with the fireflies because of Rain. Gecko asks Elephant to make Rain stop.

4

Rain tells Elephant that he makes puddles for mosquitoes. Without mosquitoes, Gecko would not have anything to eat. Elephant reminds Gecko that the whole world is connected.

Grammar: Irregular Past Tense Verbs

Irregular Verbs Game

1. To play, take turns with a partner.

2. Toss a marker onto the game board.

3. Say the past tense form of the verb you land on. Then use the verb in a sentence to tell about the past.

am	go
is	goes
are	do

© NGSP & HB

Name _____ Date _____

Go to Sleep, Gecko!

Make a character map for the characters in "Go to Sleep, Gecko!"

Character	What the Character Does	Why the Character Does It
Gecko	He complains about the fireflies.	He can't sleep.

  Share your character map with a partner. Compare what you wrote about the characters in "Go to Sleep, Gecko!"

© NGSP & HB

Fluency: Expression

Go to Sleep, Gecko!

Use this passage to practice reading with proper expression.

Gecko thought.   2

If Elephant told Rain to stop raining,   9

there would be no holes and puddles in the road.   19

If there were no holes and puddles in the road,   29

the fireflies would stop flashing their lights . . .   36

but Gecko would have nothing to eat!   43

"Gecko," said Elephant.   46

"This world is all connected.   51

Some things you just have to put up with.   60

Now go home and go to sleep."   67

Expression

B ☐ Does not read with feeling.

I ☐ Reads with some feeling, but does not match content.

A ☐ Reads with appropriate feeling for most content.

AH ☐ Reads with appropriate feeling for all content.

Accuracy and Rate Formula

Use the formula to measure a reader's accuracy and rate while reading aloud.

_____ − _____ = _____
words attempted   number of errors   words correct per minute
in one minute   (wcpm)

© NGSP & HB

Name _____ Date _____

Enric Sala: Marine Ecologist

Use Word Detective cards to write about words from the selection.

WORD DETECTIVE

New Word: _____

What I think it means: _____

_____

🔍 Clues: _____

_____

📖 Definition: _____

_____

_____

WORD DETECTIVE

New Word: _____

What I think it means: _____

_____

🔍 Clues: _____

_____

📖 Definition: _____

_____

Share a word you learned with a partner. Describe what it means.

_____

Respond and Extend: Comparison Chart

Compare Genres

Complete the comparison chart to show how the selections are the same and different.

"Go to Sleep, Gecko!"	"Enric Sala: Marine Ecologist"
• folk tale • fiction	• profile • nonfiction

💬 **Use your comparison chart to tell a partner how "Go to Sleep, Gecko!" and "Enric Sala: Marine Ecologist" are alike and different.**

© NGSP & HB

Name _____ Date _____

Gecko in the Past

Grammar Rules Past Tense Verbs

- Add *-ed* to most verbs when you talk about a past action.
  Example: *kick* + *-ed* = *kicked*
- Some verbs have special forms to show an action in the past.
  Example: *say* → *said*

Circle the correct verb form.

1. Gecko want/(wanted) to sleep that night.

2. Gecko goed/went to see Elephant.

3. Elephant talks/talked to the fireflies last week.

4. The fireflies seed/saw Elephant coming.

5. Gecko sayed/said everything was okay.

© NGSP & HB

 Use the past tense of *is* or *are* in a sentence about Gecko.

Name _____   Date _____

Go to Sleep, Gecko!

Setting: The play takes place at Elephant's house in the forest.

Cast of Characters: Narrator, Elephant, Gecko

Scene 1: At Elephant's house

Gecko is standing outside the window of a small house under a coconut tree. Through the window, Elephant can be seen sleeping.

Narrator: Late one night, Gecko went to see Elephant. Elephant was sleeping, but Gecko could not sleep.

Gecko: Geck-o! Geck-o!

Elephant *[sleepy]***:** Gecko! What are you doing here? It is the middle of the night. Go home and go to bed.

Gecko: I cannot sleep, Elephant. The fireflies are blinking their lights on and off. They are too bright. You are the village boss. You have to make them stop.

Elephant: I will talk to them tomorrow. Now go home and go to bed.

Gecko *[grumpy]***:** All right. I am going home now.

Narrator: The next day Elephant asked the fireflies why they blinked. They said Rain made holes in the road. They did not want anybody to fall into the holes.

Scene 2: At Elephant's house

Gecko is again standing outside the window of a small house in the forest. Elephant is looking at Gecko out of the window.

Narrator: That night, Gecko went to Elephant's house again. He could not sleep.

Elephant: Gecko! Go home and go to bed.

Gecko: But the fireflies are still blinking. You said you would make them stop.

Elephant: The fireflies have to blink their lights. They do not want anyone to fall into a hole in the road. You have to put up with them.

Gecko: A hole in the road? Why are there holes in the road?

Elephant: Rain makes the holes in the road.

Gecko: Make Rain stop! You are the village boss.

Elephant: I will talk to Rain tomorrow. Now go home and go to bed.

Narrator: The next day, Elephant asked Rain why he made holes in the road. Rain said that he made puddles for the mosquitoes. The mosquitoes needed puddles. And Gecko needed the mosquitoes to eat.

Scene 3: At Elephant's house

Gecko is again standing outside the window of a small house in the forest. Elephant is looking out of the window. He looks very grumpy with Gecko.

Narrator: That night, Gecko went to Elephant's house. He still could not sleep.

Elephant: Gecko! GO HOME and go to bed.

Gecko: Elephant, the fireflies are still blinking. PLEASE make them stop!

Elephant: Rain has to make puddles every afternoon. If there are no puddles, there are no mosquitoes. And if there are no mosquitoes, YOU will have nothing to eat. What do you think about that?

Narrator: Gecko thought. He did not want the fireflies to blink. But he really did not want to have nothing to eat!

Elephant: The whole world is connected, Gecko. You have to put up with some things. Now go home and go to sleep.

Narrator: So Gecko went home and went to sleep. Outside his house, the fireflies blinked their lights. In this world, you have to put up with some things.

End of play

Odd Couples

1
Life in the wild is difficult. Some animals pair up to help each other. Animals can help each other keep clean. Cleaner shrimp eat dead skin and pests off fish.

2
Some animals get a ride. The remora fish attaches to sharks. The shark gives the fish a ride. The fish eats the shark's leftover food.

3
Some animals share the same food. The honeyguide bird finds a beehive, and the ratel tears it open.

4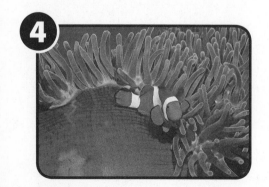
Some animals protect each other. The clownfish lives inside a sea anemone's tentacles. The sea anemone eats fish that try to eat the clownfish.

© NGSP & HB

Name _____   Date _____

What Will Happen Next?

Grammar Rules Future Tense Verbs

- A **future tense verb** tells about an action that will happen later, or in the future.

- Add **will** before a present tense verb to make a future tense verb. (Example: That **will happen** tomorrow morning.)

Circle the future tense verbs.

1. How do you think the elk (will respond) to the tiger?

2. The elk will run away from its enemy.

3. If the elk stays, the tiger will hunt it.

4. How do you think the plover will react to the crocodile?

5. The plover will go in the crocodile's mouth!

6. The crocodile will watch the plover.

7. The plover will clean the crocodile's teeth.

8. Then the plover will fly away.

 Write a new sentence using a future tense verb. Share your sentence with a partner. Have your partner identify the verb.

Name _____ Date _____

Odd Couples

1

Life in the wild is difficult. Some animals pair up to help each other. Animals can help each other keep clean. Cleaner shrimp eat dead skin and pests off fish.

2

Some animals get a ride. The remora fish attaches to sharks. The shark gives the fish a ride. The fish eats the shark's leftover food.

3

Some animals share the same food. The honeyguide bird finds a beehive, and the ratel tears it open.

4

Some animals protect each other. The clownfish lives inside a sea anemone's tentacles. The sea anemone eats fish that try to eat the clownfish.

© NGSP & HB

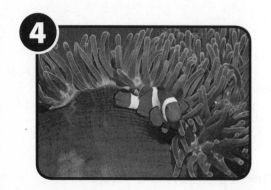

Name _____ Date _____

Forming the Future Tense

Grammar Rules Future Tense Verbs

There are two ways to make a verb tell about the future.

1. Add **will** before a present tense verb.
    (Example: I <u>will</u> call you tomorrow.)

2. Add a phrase with **going to** before a verb.

I	**<u>am</u> going to** respond.
You, We, They	**<u>are</u> going to** respond.
He, She, It	**<u>is going</u>** to respond.

Write the underlined verb another way.

1. I <u>will help</u> you with your homework. _____am going to help_____

2. You <u>will learn</u> about animal partners. _____

3. Each odd couple <u>will amaze</u> you. _____

4. Their actions <u>will surprise</u> you, too. _____

5. We <u>will have</u> fun talking about them! _____

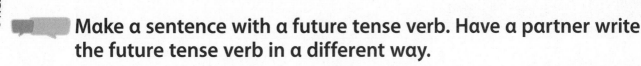 **Make a sentence with a future tense verb. Have a partner write the future tense verb in a different way.**

© NGSP & HB

Name _____   Date _____

Vocabulary: Apply Word Knowledge

Yes or No?

1. Listen to the questions. Write the Key Word where it belongs in each sentence.
2. Listen to the questions again.
3. Write **yes** or **no** for each question.

1. Do animals in the wild hide from ____danger____ ? ____yes____

2. Are cleaner shrimp and oxpeckers animal _____?
   _____

3. Can animals _____ each other? _____

4. Is a plover _____ to a honeyguide bird? _____

5. Are the clownfish and sea anemone _____ partners?
   _____

6. Does a badger have the _____ to help a coyote?
   _____

© NGSP & HB

Odd Couples

Fill out the topic and main idea chart for "Odd Couples."

Topic:	**Main Idea:** Animal partnerships help both animals survive.

Detail: Cleaner shrimp keep other fish clean.
Detail:

Use your topic and main idea chart to tell a partner about "Odd Couples."

Name _____   Date _____

Odd Couples

Use this passage to practice reading with proper intonation.

Like plovers, oxpeckers are birds. They ride on   8

giraffes, rhinos, and other big buddies.   14

The big buddies don't mind. Why not? Well, the birds   24

eat bugs. That's good for the big animals. In return,   34

the birds get plenty of food. It's a perfect pairing!   44

Intonation

B ☐ Does not change pitch.   **A** ☐ Changes pitch to match some of the content.

I ☐ Changes pitch, but does not match content.   **AH** ☐ Changes pitch to match all of the content.

Accuracy and Rate Formula

Use the formula to measure a reader's accuracy and rate while reading aloud.

_____ − _____ = _____
words attempted   number of errors   words correct per minute
  in one minute   (wcpm)

© NGSP & HB

Name _____ Date _____

Working Together

Make a K-W-L-Q chart as you read "Working Together."

K What I Know	W What I Want to Learn	L What I Learned	Q Questions I Still Have

 Share your chart with a partner. Talk about how to find answers to the questions you still have after reading.

Name _____   Date _____

Compare Topics and Main Ideas

Complete the comparison chart to compare "Odd Couples" and "Working Together."

Title	Topic	Main Idea
"Odd Couples"		
"Working Together"		

 Use the comparison chart to explain the topic and main idea of each selection.

© NGSP & HB

Grammar: Future Tense

Make-It-Future Tense Game

1. **Play with a partner.**
2. **Spin the spinner.**
3. **Change the verb to show the future tense. Say a sentence using the future tense verb.**

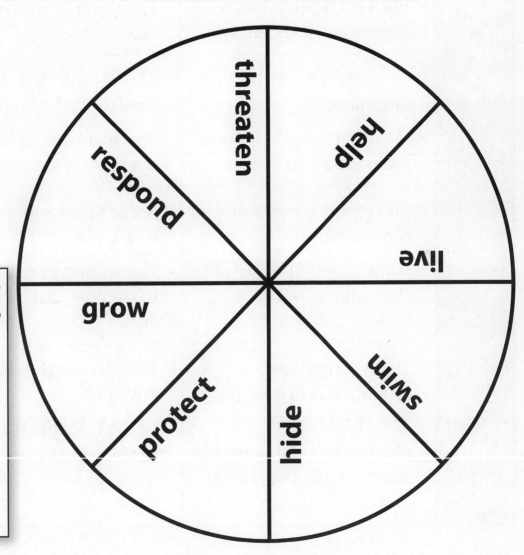

Make a Spinner

1. Push a paper clip in the center of the circle.

2. Hold one end of the paper clip with a pencil.

3. Spin the paper clip around the pencil.

Name _____ Date _____

Organization

	Is the report well organized?	Do the ideas in the report flow well?
4 Wow!	• The report is very well organized. • Each paragraph has a main idea and details.	• The writing in the report is very smooth. • Each idea flows smoothly into the next.
3 Ahh.	• The report is mostly well organized. • Most paragraphs have a main idea and details.	• Most of the ideas in the report flow well. • There are only a few places where the writing jumps around.
2 Hmm.	• The report is not that well organized. • Some paragraphs are not clear and do not have enough details.	• Some ideas in the report do not flow well. • The writing jumps from one idea to another, but I can follow it a little.
1 Huh?	• The writing is not organized and does not look like a report. • Maybe the writer forgot to use the topic, main idea, and details chart.	• The ideas in the report do not flow well • I can't tell what the writer wants to say.

Name _____   Date _____

Topic, Main Idea, and Details Chart

Complete the chart for your report.

Topic:	
Main Idea 1:	**Details:**
Main Idea 2:	**Details:**
Main Idea 3:	**Details:**
Main Idea 4:	**Details:**

© NGSP & HB

Revise

Use the Revising Marks to revise the paragraph. Look for:
- details that support main ideas
- an order that makes sense

Revising Marks	
∧	Add.
℘	Take out.
⌒⌐	Move to here.

Crocodiles and Plovers

Plovers are small birds. They are not afraid of crocodiles.

A crocodile opens its mouth, and a plover hops in. The plover eats the food stuck in the crocodile's teeth.

Crocodiles have teeth. Food gets stuck in their teeth.

Now the crocodile has a clean mouth!

Edit and Proofread

Use the Editing Marks to edit and proofread this report. Look for:
- **commas after introductory words and phrases**
- **future tense with *going to* and *will***
- **correct spelling**

Editing Marks	
∧	Add.
⌘	Take out.
⬯	Check spelling.
⌄	Add comma.

The Ratel and the Honeyguide

Ratels and honeyguides don't look like partners. However they help each other get their favorite food — honey! What are these creatures? Ratels are mammals and are also known as "honey badgers." and Honeyguides are birds.

First the bird will flies over grasslands looking for beehives. When it sees a hive, it make noise.

If the ratel has heared the noise, it will rush to the hive. It uses its sharp claws to tear open the hive. Sadly this is not good for the bees.

The ratel and bird work well together. When they do, they know they is goings to have a good meal!

Unit Concept Map

Our United States

Make a concept map with the answers to the Big Question: What does America mean to you?

America means many things to many people.

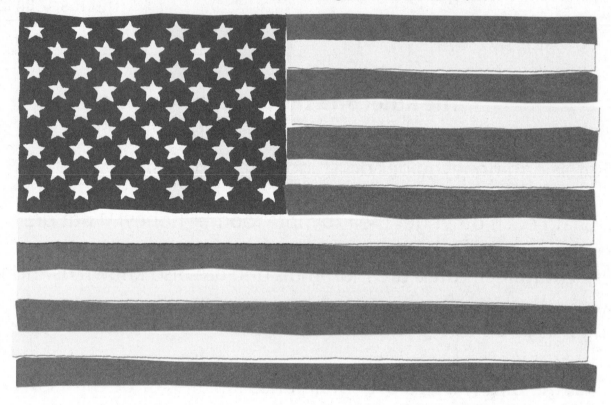

Name _____ Date _____

Character's Feelings

Make a character map to tell how a character feels and why.

Character	How the Character Feels	Why the Character Feels This Way

 Use your character map to tell a partner about a character's feelings in a story that you like.

Name _____ Date _____

Where Are They?

Grammar Rules Prepositions

Prepositions tell where objects are.

Example: *The hamburgers are on a plate.*

1. Color objects that are <u>on</u> the table yellow.

2. Color objects that are <u>under</u> the table blue.

3. Color the object that is <u>beside</u> the table green.

4. Color the object that is <u>above</u> the table red.

 Use prepositions to tell a partner where things are.

© NGSP & HB

Name _____   Date _____

Apple Pie Fourth of July

A family's store is open on the Fourth of July. The girl's parents cook Chinese noodles. The girl says no one wants Chinese food on the Fourth of July.

The parade passes the store. Customers buy soda and chips. They buy ice cream, ice, and matches. The girl says no one wants Chinese food on the Fourth of July.

The girl eats the noodles. Her parents don't understand that Americans don't eat Chinese food on the Fourth of July.

Many hungry customers come for Chinese food. Finally the family closes the store to watch the fireworks and eat apple pie.

Name _____   Date _____

Spin and Move Game

1. Play with a partner.

2. Spin the spinner.

3. Say the word and use classroom objects to act out where things move.

4. The first player to correctly say and act out all six movements wins.

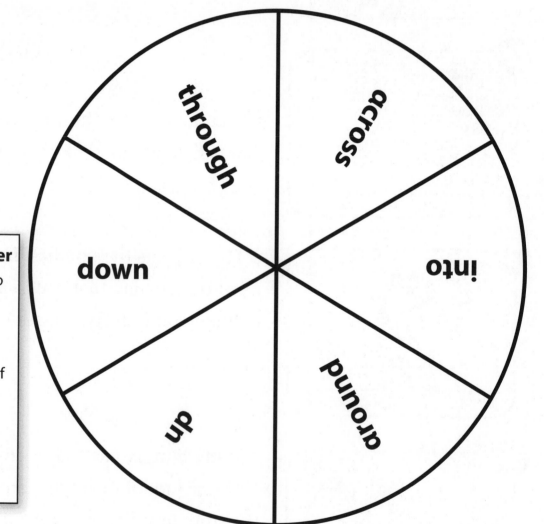

Make a Spinner

1. Put a paper clip in the center of the circle.

2. Hold one end of the paper clip with a pencil.

3. Spin the paper clip around the object.

© NGSP & HB

Name _____   Date _____

Apple Pie 4th of July

Make a character map for the characters in "Apple Pie 4th of July."

Character	How the Character Feels	Why the Character Feels This Way
The girl telling the story	Unhappy	She thinks no one will want Chinese food on the 4th of July.

Use your character map to describe the story characters to a partner.

Fluency: Intonation

Use this passage to practice reading with proper intonation.

Apple Pie 4th of July

I tell them no one—no one—came,	8
so we ate it up ourselves	14
but the customers smell the food in the	22
kitchen now—	24
and Mother walks through the	29
swinging door	31
holding a tray of chicken chow mein	38
and Father follows her	42
step for step	45
with a brand-new pan of	50
sweet-and-sour pork—	52
and three more people get in line,	59
eleven more at six o'clock,	64
nine at seven,	67
twelve by eight,	70
more and more and more and more	77
until it's time to close the store—	84
time to climb to our rooftop chairs,	91
way up high, beyond the crowd,	97
where we sit and watch the fireworks show—	105
and eat our apple pie.	110

Intonation

B ☐ Does not change pitch.   A ☐ Changes pitch to match some of the content.

I ☐ Changes pitch, but does not match content.   AH ☐ Changes pitch to match all of the content.

Accuracy and Rate Formula

Use the formula to measure a reader's accuracy and rate while reading aloud.

_____ − _____ = _____
words attempted   number of errors   words corrected per
in one minute   minute (wcpm)

© NGSP & HB

Name _____   Date _____

Compare Language

Compare the language in "Apple Pie 4th of July" and "America: A Weaving." Write what the sentences or phrases mean.

"Apple Pie 4th of July"	"America: A Weaving"
I hear the parade passing by. *This means exactly what it says.*	America, America, a never-ending weaving! *Meaning: Many cultures and traditions make America.*
My parents do not understand all American things.	

 Take turns with a partner. Explain which words mean exactly what they say and which words do not.

© NGSP & HB

Grammar: Prepositions

An American Restaurant

Grammar Rules Prepositions

Some prepositions show location.
Examples: in, on, above, over, below, under, beside, next to

Some prepositions show direction.
Examples: up, down, through, across, into, around

Circle the word to complete each sentence. Then read the sentence.

1. The pot is under/on the stove.

2. Dad puts noodles into/across the pot.

3. I stand next to/above Dad.

4. I stir the noodles around/down with a spoon.

5. The flag is beside/through the stove.

💬 **Write a sentence that includes a preposition. Share your sentence with a partner.**

© NGSP & HB

Author's Purpose

Make an author's purpose chart to tell about a nonfiction text you have read.

Clues from the Title:	**Clues from the Kind of Writing:**
Author's Purpose	
Clues from the Details:	**Clues from the Main Idea:**

Share your chart with a partner and compare the author's purpose.

Grammar: Prepositions That Show Time

Happy Fourth of July!

Grammar Rules Prepositions

A **preposition** can tell when something happens.

• We went to the National Park **before** summer.

• We went hiking **after** the sunrise.

• We ate trail mix **during** our hike.

Circle the preposition in each sentence.

1. We celebrate America's birthday in July.

2. Independence Day is on July 4th.

3. We pack a picnic before the celebration.

4. My family meets at seven o'clock.

5. We eat dinner during sunset.

6. Then we watch fireworks after dark.

7. It is another year until the next celebration.

 Choose a sentence and change the preposition. Share your new sentence with a partner. Tell how the new preposition changes the meaning of the sentence.

© NGSP & HB

Name _____   Date _____

America is . . .

1

America is our country. The name of our nation means freedom to many people all over the world.

2

America is fifty states that stretch from the Atlantic Ocean to the Pacific Ocean. America is a flag of fifty stars and thirteen stripes.

3

America is millions of people doing different jobs. It is the country and the cities, the mountains, and the deserts.

4

America is a land where people are free to speak out. They can worship and work. They can play and follow their dreams.

© NGSP & HB

Tell More

Grammar Rules Prepositional Phrases

A **prepositional phrase** tells more about something in the sentence.
- It begins with a preposition.
- It ends with a noun or a pronoun.

Underline the prepositional phrase in each sentence. Circle each preposition.

1. America has many national holidays (during) the year.

2. We celebrate Martin Luther King, Jr.'s, birthday in January.

3. President's Day is in February.

4. Memorial Day became a holiday after the American Civil War.

5. Most schools start summer vacation before July 4th.

6. Then there is not another holiday until September.

7. People celebrate Labor Day with parades.

8. All of us are grateful at Thanksgiving.

 Choose a sentence and change the prepositional phrase. Share your new sentence with a partner.

© NGSP & HB

America Is...

Make an author's purpose chart. Figure out the author's purpose for writing "America Is ...."

Clues from the Title:

"America Is..."
The selection is about America.

Clues from the Kind of Writing:

Literary nonfiction presents facts and ideas in an interesting way.

Author's Purpose

Clues from the Details:

Clues from the Main Idea

💬 **Work with a partner. Compare the author's purposes that you found.**

Fluency: Phrasing

Use this passage to practice reading with proper phrasing.

America Is...

America is tall skyscrapers with many	6
windows that go up, up, up. It is the people	16
in cities who rush to and from work in cars,	26
buses, and taxicabs, and on subways and	33
fast trains. From New York City to Los	40
Angeles, this is America.	44

Phrasing

B ☐ Rarely pauses while reading the text.   A ☐ Frequently pauses at appropriate points in the text.

I ☐ Occasionally pauses while reading the text.   AH ☐ Consistently pauses at all appropriate points in the text.

Accuracy and Rate Formula

Use the formula to measure a reader's accuracy and rate while reading aloud.

$$\underset{\substack{\text{words attempted} \\ \text{in one minute}}}{\underline{\hspace{3cm}}} - \underset{\text{number of errors}}{\underline{\hspace{3cm}}} = \underset{\substack{\text{words corrected per} \\ \text{minute (wcpm)}}}{\underline{\hspace{3cm}}}$$

Name _____ Date _____

This Land Is Your Land

On each card, write an unfamiliar word, what you think it means, and clues to its meaning.

WORD DETECTIVE

New Word: _____

What I think it means: _____

_____

Clues: _____

_____

Definition: _____

_____

_____

WORD DETECTIVE

New Word: _____

What I think it means: _____

_____

Clues: _____

_____

Definition: _____

After you have finished reading, use a dictionary to find the definition of the word. Share your work with a partner.

© NGSP & HB

Name _____ Date _____

Compare Author's Purpose

Make a comparison chart. Show how "America Is..." and "This Land Is Your Land" are the same and how they are different.

	"America Is..." by Louise Borden	"This Land Is Your Land" by Woody Guthrie
persuade readers		✓
inform readers	✓	
entertain readers		
share experiences		
express feelings		
express creativity		

 Share your chart with a partner. Take turns comparing the authors' purposes in each selection.

© NGSP & HB

Grammar: Prepositional Phrases

Do These Details Fit?

1. Partner 1 points to a sentence.

2. Partner 2 points to a prepositional phrase.

3. If the cards make a clear sentence, color in the squares. If not, begin again.

4. Play until all the squares are colored.

Sentences

Sentence Starters

We go _____.	Teresa and I write _____.	Koji and Lynn have fun _____.	You and I read _____.

Prepositional Phrases

to the park	after breakfast	during the concert	into the monument
along the coast	with the map	about American history	under the blue sky

Writing Project: Rubric

Voice and Style

	Does the writing sound real?	Do the words fit the purpose and audience?
4 Wow!	• The writing shows who the writer is. • The writer seems to be talking right to me.	• The writer uses words that really fit the audience and purpose.
3 Ahh.	• The writing shows who the writer is. • The writer seems to care about the ideas in the writing.	• The writer uses good words for the audience and purpose.
2 Hmm.	• It's hard to tell who the writer is. • The writer doesn't seem to be talking to me.	• The writer uses some words that fit the audience and purpose.
1 Huh?	• I can't tell who the writer is. • The writer doesn't seem to care.	• The words don't fit the audience or purpose.

Name _____ Date _____

Feelings Chart

Complete the chart for your personal narrative.

Person	How the Person Feels	Why the Person Feels This Way

Revise

Use the Revising Marks to revise the paragraph. Look for:

- words and sentences that sound like you
- details that tell why the event was important

Revising Marks	
^	Add.
ℱ	Take out.

Our Class Party

A few weeks ago, my class had a party. People brought food

that their families had made. I brought some things and my friends

brought some other things. The food all smelled amazing, and

I felt. There was food there that I had never seen before.

This party was important to me. It showed me that people from

the United States may come from many different cultures but here

we become one culture, like different foods from different countries

became one meal for my class.

© NGSP & HB

Name _____   Date _____

Writing Project

Edit and Proofread

Use the Editing Marks to edit and
proofread the personal narrative.
Look for:

- misspelled words
- paragraph indents
- correct prepositions and
  prepositional phrases

Editing Marks	
∧	Add.
℘	Take out.
⬭	Check spelling.
⌐	Indent.

A New Life in America

My class went to Ellis Island. Until 1954 Ellis Island was where many

people first entered America. We learned about all the people who

came by America looking for freedom.

Many of these people had no money. All of there possessions

were under one or too suitcases. They could not read or rite English,

America is a place where people can start a new life. That's what

America means to me.

Acknowledgments

Acknowledgments
Grateful acknowledgment is given to the authors, artists, photographers, museums, publishers, and agents for permission to reprint copyrighted material. Every effort has been made to secure the appropriate permission. If any omissions have been made or if corrections are required, please contact the Publisher.

Children's Book Press: From *Quinito's Neighborhood/El Vecindario de Quinito* by Ina Cumpiano, illustrated by José Ramírez. Text copyright © 2005 Children's Book Press. Illustrations © 2009 by José Ramírez. Reprinted by permission of the publisher, Children's Book Press, San Francisco, Calif., www.childrensbookpress.org.

Star Bright Books, Inc.: From *Twilight Hunt* by Narelle Oliver. Copyright © 2002 by Narelle Oliver. Reprinted by permission of the publisher, Star Bright Books, Inc.

HarperCollins Publishers: From *When the Wind Stops* by Charlotte Zolotow, illustrated by Stefano Vitale. Text copyright © 1962, 1995 by Charlotte Zolotow, illustrations © by Stefano Vitale. Reprinted by permission of HarperCollins Publishers.

Penguin Group (USA) Inc.: From *What Makes the Seasons?* by Megan Montague Cash. Copyright © 2003 by Megan Montague Cash. Reprinted by permission of Penguin Group (USA) Inc.

Marian Reiner: From *Go to Sleep, Gecko* by Margaret Read MacDonald, illustrated by Geraldo Valério. Text copyright © 2006 by Margaret Read MacDonald. Illustrations © 2006 by Geraldo Valério. Published by August House Publishers Inc. Used by permission of Marian Reiner.

Houghton Mifflin Harcourt: From *Apple Pie 4th of July* by Janet S. Wong, pictures by Margaret Chodos-Irvine. Copyright © 2002 by Janet S. Wong. Illustrations © 2002 by Margaret Chodos-Irvine. Reprinted by permission of Houghton Mifflin Harcourt Publishing Company. All rights reserved.

Simon and Schuster, Inc.: From *America is...* by Louise Borden, illustrated by Stacey Schuett. Copyright © 2002 by Louise Borden. Illustrations © 2002 by Stacey Schuett. Reprinted by permission of Simon and Schuster, Inc.

Photographic Credits
205a (tr) Corbis

Illustrator Credits
Dartmouth Publishing, Inc.

The National Geographic Society
John M. Fahey, Jr., President & Chief Executive Officer
Gilbert M. Grosvenor, Chairman of the Board